はしがき

　本書は第一学習社発行の英語教科書「Vivid English Communication Ⅱ」に完全準拠したワークブックです。本課は各パート見開き2ページで，教科書本文を使って「聞く」「読む」「話す（やり取り）」「話す（発表）」「書く」の4技能5領域の力を育成する問題をバランスよく用意しました。

本書の構成と利用法

JN102754

【教科書本文】

- ●新出単語を太字で示しました。
- ●教科書に印字されていない部分（リスニングスクリプト）には網かけして示しています。
- ●意味のまとまりごとにスラッシュを入れました。ここで示した意味のまとまりや，英語の強弱のリズムやイントネーションなどに注意して，本文を流暢に音読できるようにしましょう。「スピーキング・トレーナー」を使って，自分の発言を後から確認したり，発話の流暢さ（1分あたりの発話語数：words per minute）を算出することができます。発話の流暢さは70〜110wpm を目指しましょう。

Reading

- ●大学入学共通テストなどの形式に対応した，本文の内容理解問題です。

Vocabulary & Grammar

- ●英検®や GTEC®の形式に対応した，本文中の単語，表現，文法事項についての問題です。

Listening

- ●本文内容やテーマに関連した英文の聞き取り問題です。大学入学共通テストの形式に対応しています。
- ●🔊は別売の音声 CD のトラック番号を示します。二次元コードを読み取って，音声を PC やスマートフォンなどから聞くこともできます。

Interaction

- ●本文内容やテーマに関連した会話などを聞いて，最後に投げかけられた質問に対して自分の考えなどを応答し，やり取りを完成させる発話問題です。

Production

- ●本文を読んだ感想や，自分の考えや意見などを話したり書いたりして伝える問題です。

◆「知識・技能」や「思考力・判断力・表現力」を養成することを意識し，設問ごとに主に対応する観点を示しました。
◆ライティング，スピーキング問題を自分で採点できるようにしています。
　別冊『解答・解説集』の「ルーブリック評価表」（ある観点における学習の到達度を判断する基準）を用いて，自分の記述内容や発言内容を採点できます。

CONTENTS

CAN-DO List
知識・技能

☐進行形, 受け身, S + V + C (＝現在分詞・過去分詞)や, 語・連語・慣用表現について理解を深め, これらを適切に活用することができる。
☐強弱のリズムを理解して音読することができる。

☐seem to ～, It is ... (for A) to ～, 強調や, 語・連語・慣用表現について理解を深め, これらを適切に活用することができる。
☐強弱のリズムを理解して音読することができる。

☐It is ＋形容詞＋ that-節, 完了形, 完了形(受け身)や, 語・連語・慣用表現について理解を深め, これらを適切に活用することができる。
☐強弱のリズムを理解して音読することができる。

☐S + V + O + O (＝名詞節), 関係代名詞(制限用法・非制限用法)や, 語・連語・慣用表現について理解を深め, これらを適切に活用することができる。
☐イントネーションを理解して音読することができる。

☐群動詞(受け身), 進行形(受け身), 関係副詞(制限用法・非制限用法)や, 語・連語・慣用表現について理解を深め, これらを適切に活用することができる。
☐イントネーションを理解して音読することができる。

☐文構造・文法事項や, 語・連語・慣用表現について理解を深め, これらを適切に活用することができる。
☐イントネーションを理解して音読することができる。

☐「時」や「理由」などを表す副詞節, 分詞構文(現在分詞), 「推量」を表す助動詞, 助動詞＋ have ＋過去分詞や, 語・連語・慣用表現について理解を深め, これらを適切に活用することができる。
☐イントネーションを理解して音読することができる。

☐「時」や「理由」などを表す副詞節, 分詞構文(過去分詞), 関係代名詞 ... 前置詞, 前置詞＋関係代名詞や, 語・連語・慣用表現について理解を深め, これらを適切に活用することができる。
☐音の変化を理解して音読することができる。

☐倒置, S + V + O + C (＝原形不定詞・現在分詞・過去分詞), 同格の that や, 語・連語・慣用表現について理解を深め, これらを適切に活用することができる。
☐音の変化を理解して音読することができる。

☐省略, 完了不定詞, All you have to do is (to) ～, 仮定法や, 語・連語・慣用表現について理解を深め, これらを適切に活用することができる。
☐シャドーイングをすることができる。

☐倒置, 分詞構文(完了形), as if ＋仮定法, 複合関係詞や, 語・連語・慣用表現について理解を深め, これらを適切に活用することができる。
☐シャドーイングをすることができる。

☐文構造・文法事項や, 語・連語・慣用表現について理解を深め, これらを適切に活用することができる。
☐シャドーイングをすることができる。

☐文構造・文法事項や, 語・連語・慣用表現について理解を深め, これらを適切に活用することができる。
☐シャドーイングをすることができる。

思考力・判断力・表現力

- ☐ 📖 日本人アスリートと英語について的確に理解し，その内容を整理することができる。
- ☐ 🎧 スポーツや英語学習に関する短い英文を聞いて，必要な情報を把握することができる。
- ☐ 🗣 スポーツや英語学習について，適切に情報や考えを伝え合うことができる。
- ☐ ✍ 英語学習やスピーチや部活動について，自分の考えを書いて伝えることができる。

- ☐ 📖 バナナの特徴や危機について的確に理解し，その内容を整理することができる。
- ☐ 🎧 バナナに関する短い英文を聞いて，必要な情報を把握することができる。
- ☐ 🗣 バナナや農業について，適切に情報や考えを伝え合うことができる。
- ☐ ✍ 好きな料理や農業について，自分の考えを書いて伝えることができる。

- ☐ 📖 自然災害と防災について的確に理解し，その内容を整理することができる。
- ☐ 🎧 自然災害や防災に関する短い英文を聞いて，必要な情報を把握することができる。
- ☐ 🗣 自然災害について，適切に情報や考えを伝え合うことができる。
- ☐ ✍ 自然災害や防災について，自分の考えを書いて伝えることができる。

- ☐ 📖 国際化について的確に理解し，その内容を整理することができる。
- ☐ 🎧 国際化に関する短い英文を聞いて，必要な情報を把握することができる。
- ☐ 🗣 留学や国際化について，適切に情報や考えを伝え合うことができる。
- ☐ 🗣 国際化について，自分の考えを話して伝えることができる。
- ☐ ✍ 日本文化や国際化について，自分の考えを書いて伝えることができる。

- ☐ 📖 ネコのくぅと犬のしののきずなについて的確に理解し，その内容を整理することができる。
- ☐ 🎧 動物や友達や落ち込んだときに関する短い英文を聞いて，必要な情報を把握することができる。
- ☐ 🗣 本や幸せや動物や将来の職業について，適切に情報や考えを伝え合うことができる。
- ☐ 🗣 友達について，自分の考えを話して伝えることができる。
- ☐ ✍ 動物や落ち込んだときについて，自分の考えを書いて伝えることができる。

- ☐ 📖 ストーリーの展開を的確に理解し，その内容を整理することができる。

- ☐ 📖 ドローンのメリット・問題点や今後の展望について的確に理解し，その内容を整理することができる。
- ☐ 🎧 ドローンに関する短い英文を聞いて，必要な情報を把握することができる。
- ☐ 🗣 ドローンについて，適切に情報や考えを伝え合うことができる。
- ☐ 🗣 ドローンについて，自分の考えを話して伝えることができる。
- ☐ ✍ ドローンについて，自分の考えを書いて伝えることができる。

- ☐ 📖 スーパークローン文化財の役割や重要性について的確に理解し，その内容を整理することができる。
- ☐ 🎧 文化財や芸術に関する短い英文を聞いて，必要な情報を把握することができる。
- ☐ 🗣 文化財や芸術やクローン技術について，適切に情報や考えを伝え合うことができる。
- ☐ 🗣 好きな画家について，自分の考えを話して伝えることができる。
- ■ ✍ 文化財や芸術やクローン技術について，自分の考えを書いて伝えることができる。

- ☐ 📖 平和のメッセージについて的確に理解し，その内容を整理することができる。
- ☐ 🎧 平和に関する短い英文を聞いて，必要な情報を把握することができる。
- ☐ 🗣 スピーチや戦争について，適切に情報や考えを伝え合うことができる。
- ☐ ✍ 戦争や会いたい人物について，自分の考えを書いて伝えることができる。

- ☐ 📖 地域社会への参画や貢献について的確に理解し，その内容を整理することができる。
- ☐ 🎧 地域社会や将来や部活動に関する短い英文を聞いて，必要な情報を把握することができる。
- ☐ 🗣 競技大会や地域社会について，適切に情報や考えを伝え合うことができる。
- ☐ 🗣 地域社会について，自分の考えを話して伝えることができる。
- ☐ ✍ 行事や地域社会や将来について，自分の考えを書いて伝えることができる。

- ☐ 📖 ワイルドライフツーリズムについて的確に理解し，その内容を整理することができる。
- ☐ 🎧 SNSや休暇の予定やワイルドライフツーリズムに関する短い英文を聞いて，必要な情報を把握することができる。
- ☐ 🗣 動物や修学旅行やSNSについて，適切に情報や考えを伝え合うことができる。
- ☐ ✍ 動物やワイルドライフツーリズムについて，自分の考えを書いて伝えることができる。

- ☐ 📖 ストーリーの展開を的確に理解し，その内容を整理することができる。

- ☐ 📖 英文の内容を的確に理解し，整理することができる。

Japanese Athletes and English

Today, / many Japanese athletes are playing sports / in various countries / around the world. // They show us great performances, / and some of them are also **proficient** in English. // One of those athletes / is Rui Hachimura, / an NBA player. //

5 In high school, / Rui was not good at English. // In his third year, / he decided / to play basketball / at an American university. // From that time, / he continued / to study English very hard. //

At university, / Rui took an ESL course. // **Furthermore**, / he discovered his own English-learning method. // One day, / while he was listening / to English

10 **rap** songs, / he started / trying to **pronounce** the words / as they sounded. // Then, / he repeated this / again and again. // Rui speaks **fluent** English now. //

(115 words)

音読しよう   スピーキング・トレーナー

Practice 1 スラッシュ位置で文を区切って読んでみよう ☐
Practice 2 英語の強弱のリズムに注意して読んでみよう ☐
TRY! 1分30秒以内に本文全体を音読しよう ☐

Reading 本文の内容を読んで理解しよう【知識・技能】【思考力・判断力・表現力】   共通テスト GTEC®

Make the correct choice to complete each sentence or answer each question. (各5点)

(1) What does "pronounce" mean in line 10? ☐
　① To listen to what other people are saying.
　② To learn something so that you will remember it exactly.
　③ To make the sound of a word or letter.
　④ To read something silently to oneself.

(2) Many Japanese athletes ☐.
　① are internationally successful
　② are playing basketball as NBA players
　③ are studying English very hard
　④ want to play sports in the U.S.

(3) In high school, Rui ☐.
　① listened to English rap songs again and again
　② made up his mind to play basketball in the U.S.
　③ took an ESL course
　④ was proficient in English

Goals

🔊 英語の強弱のリズムを理解して音読することができる。　📖 八村選手に関する英文を読んで概要や要点をとらえることができる。
💬 文脈を理解して適切な語句を用いて英文を完成することができる。　🎧 平易な英語で話される短い英文を聞いて必要な情報を聞き取ることができる。
💬 好きなスポーツについて簡単な語句を用いて情報や考えを伝えることができる。　✍ 英語学習について簡単な語句を用いて考えを表現することができる。

🃏 Vocabulary & Grammar　重要表現や文法事項について理解しよう【知識】　英検® GTEC®

Make the correct choice to complete each sentence. （各3点）

(1) It is often said Europeans are proficient (　　　) several foreign languages.
　① about　　　　② for　　　　③ in　　　　④ of

(2) When I was a child, I was not good (　　　) sports.
　① at　　　　② in　　　　③ to　　　　④ with

(3) Since Mary has lived in Japan for ten years, she can speak (　　　) Japanese.
　① different　　② differently　　③ fluent　　④ fluently

(4) The play was not very good; (　　　), the actors were not well prepared.
　① although　　② eventually　　③ furthermore　　④ so

(5) The boys broke a window when they (　　　) soccer.
　① are playing　　② play　　③ was playing　　④ were playing

🎧 Listening　英文を聞いて理解しよう【知識・技能】【思考力・判断力・表現力】　共通テスト　💿 2

Listen to the English and make the best choice to match the content. （4点）

　① In Japan, sports are becoming less popular.
　② Japanese athletes are popular overseas.
　③ Many Japanese athletes are foreign-based.

💬 Interaction　英文を聞いて会話を続けよう【知識・技能】【思考力・判断力・表現力】　スピーキング・トレーナー　💿 3

Listen to the English and respond to the last remark. （7点）

　〔メ モ　　　　　　　　　　　　　　　　　　　　　　　　　　　　　　　　　　　　　〕

🌡 **Hints**
play soccer [baseball, tennis] (サッカー[野球, テニス]をする), do judo [karate] (柔道[空手]をする)

✍ Production（Writing）　自分の考えを書いて伝えよう【思考力・判断力・表現力】

Write your answer to the following question. （9点）
What is your own English-learning method?

🌡 **Hints**
keep a diary in English (英語で日記をつける), listen to Western music (洋楽を聞く),
watch foreign dramas and movies (海外のドラマや映画をみる)

*In 2018, / Shohei was awarded / the **Rookie** of the Year Award. // He attended a party / with other prize winners, / and he said the following words / in his speech. //*

I am honored / to share this stage / with so many great players. // Congratulations to you all. // I would like to say some special thank-yous. //

5　To the **entire** Angels organization / for their **unconditional** support / and believing in me and my **vision**. // To my teammates / for their support and **encouragement**. // To my parents / for coming / from Japan / to be here / tonight. // Lastly, / to all the Angels fans, / thank you. //

Hopefully, / I will not need this **cheat sheet** / the next time I'm up here. //
10　Thank you. //

(111 words)

🔊)) **音読しよう** 📖　　　　　　　　　　　　　スピーキング・トレーナー

Practice 1　スラッシュ位置で文を区切って読んでみよう ☐
Practice 2　英語の強弱のリズムに注意して読んでみよう ☐
TRY!　1分30秒以内に本文全体を音読しよう ☐

📖 Reading　本文の内容を読んで理解しよう【知識・技能】【思考力・判断力・表現力】　　共通テスト

Make the correct choice to complete each sentence or answer each question.　(各5点)

(1) What did Shohei do with other prize winners?　☐
　① He attended a party.
　② He enjoyed having a chat in English.
　③ He listened to a speech by the U.S. President.
　④ He made a cheat sheet.

(2) Shohei expressed his thanks to ☐.
　① his brothers for coming from Japan
　② his team for its limited support
　③ his teammates for their support and encouragement
　④ the Angels fans for coming to the party

(3) Which of the following is true?　☐
　① Shohei didn't need a cheat sheet because he had memorized his entire speech.
　② Shohei expressed his regrets in his speech.
　③ Shohei's parents were so busy that they couldn't attend the party.
　④ Shohei received the Rookie of the Year Award in 2018.

Vocabulary & Grammar 重要表現や文法事項について理解しよう【知識】 英検® GTEC®

Make the correct choice to complete each sentence. （各3点）

(1) Prizes will be (　　　) to the top three runners.
　① awarded　　　　② consumed　　　　③ encouraged　　　④ produced

(2) The poet had a (　　　) of a world without war.
　① donation　　　　② result　　　　　③ trend　　　　　④ vision

(3) Tom shared his thoughts (　　　) me after the meeting.
　① at　　　　　　　② for　　　　　　③ on　　　　　　④ with

(4) I (　　　) the wedding at the church.
　① attended　　　　② mastered　　　　③ printed　　　　④ united

(5) The bad mood of the meeting (　　　).
　① not was improve　② not was improved　③ was not improve　④ was not improved

Listening 英文を聞いて理解しよう【知識・技能】【思考力・判断力・表現力】 共通テスト ● 4

Listen to the English and make the best choice to match the content. （4点）
　① The speaker plays baseball.
　② The speaker used to be a pitcher on the baseball team.
　③ The speaker wants to be a professional baseball player.

Interaction 英文を聞いて会話を続けよう【知識・技能】【思考力・判断力・表現力】 スピーキング・トレーナー ● 5

Listen to the English and respond to the last remark. （7点）
〔メ モ　　　　　　　　　　　　　　　　　　　　　　　　　　　　　　　　　　　　　〕

🔑 **Hints**
become mentally strong (精神的に強くなる), do a lot of training (トレーニングを十分に積む), skill (技術)

Production (Writing) 自分の考えを書いて伝えよう【思考力・判断力・表現力】

Write your answer to the following question. （9点）
What do you think is important to give a good speech?

🔑 **Hints**
gesture (身振り), practice in advance (事前に練習する), speak loudly and clearly (大きな声で明確に話す)

When you hear Japanese athletes' English, / you may be **concerned** / about their **pronunciation**. // However, / something else is even more important: / how **attractive** their messages are. //

Take Shohei's speech, / for example. // He did not talk / only about himself. // 5 At the beginning, / he **congratulated** the other award winners. // They were also recognized / for their great performances, / so he showed his respect / to those players. // Then, / Shohei expressed his **gratitude** / to the team, / fans / and his parents. // At the end, / he even made a joke! //

Probably, / most of you work hard / on your club activities / and English 10 learning, / just like many Japanese athletes. // Keep trying / to improve your skills / in your clubs / and your **ability** / to **command** English. //

(115 words)

🔊)) 音読しよう 📖 〰〰〰〰〰〰〰〰〰〰〰〰 スピーキング・トレーナー

Practice 1 スラッシュ位置で文を区切って読んでみよう ☐
Practice 2 英語の強弱のリズムに注意して読んでみよう ☐
TRY! 1分30秒以内に本文全体を音読しよう ☐

Reading 本文の内容を読んで理解しよう【知識・技能】【思考力・判断力・表現力】   共通テスト GTEC®

Make the correct choice to complete each sentence or answer each question. (各5点)

(1) In his speech, Shohei ☐.

① said thanks to the team, fans and his parents

② showed his respect to other players who didn't get awards

③ talked only about himself

④ told people that he was worried about his English pronunciation

(2) What does "command" mean in line 11? ☐

① ban

② control

③ demand

④ perform

(3) You have learned that ☐.

① it is important to talk about yourself in your speech

② it is the most important thing to pronounce English correctly

③ you should keep trying to improve your English

④ you should master English so that you can tell jokes in English

🎴 Vocabulary & Grammar　重要表現や文法事項について理解しよう【知識】　英検® GTEC®

Make the correct choice to complete each sentence.　(各3点)

(1) My boss (　　　) me warmly on my promotion.
　① congratulated　② effected　③ organized　④ put

(2) I'm very concerned (　　　) your future.
　① about　② of　③ on　④ to

(3) Chocolate is very (　　　) to children.
　① attractive　② crazy　③ hateful　④ official

(4) Lack of sleep may cause you to lose your (　　　) to work.
　① absence　② ability　③ behavior　④ character

(5) The movie actor sat (　　　) by his fans.
　① surround　② surrounded　③ surrounding　④ was surrounded

🎧 Listening　英文を聞いて理解しよう【知識・技能】【思考力・判断力・表現力】　共通テスト 🎵6

Listen to the English and make the best choice to match the content.　(4点)

　① The speaker likes to listen to Western music.
　② The speaker often goes to the movies when she is free.
　③ The speaker works on improving her English listening skills.

💬 Interaction　英文を聞いて会話を続けよう【知識・技能】【思考力・判断力・表現力】　スピーキング・トレーナー 🎵7

Listen to the English and respond to the remarks.　(7点)

〔メモ　　　　　　　　　　　　　　　　　　　　　　　　　　　　　　　　　　　　　〕

🔑 **Hints**
electronic dictionary (電子辞書)，paper dictionary (紙の辞書)，suitable (適している)

✍ Production (Writing)　自分の考えを書いて伝えよう【思考力・判断力・表現力】

Write your answer to the following question.　(9点)

Introduce your own or your friend's club activities.

🔑 **Hints**
所属する部活動，活動日時，活動内容などについて書きましょう。

> People around the world / seem to love bananas. // In the Philippines, / sweet **fried** bananas / are a common street food. // Puerto Ricans make a hot banana soup. // It is made / with some **seasonings**, / such as salt / and black **pepper**. // Different cultures have their own different ways / of eating this delicious fruit. //
>
> 5 Bananas are good / for our health / as well as delicious. // They **contain** a good amount of **vitamins** and **minerals**. // One of the minerals / is **potassium**. // This mineral is useful / in lowering **blood pressure**. //
>
> Bananas are very **familiar** / to people / all over the world. // However, / this fruit is in danger / of **extinction** / due to a disease. //
>
> (105 words)

 音読しよう

スピーキング・トレーナー

Practice 1 スラッシュ位置で文を区切って読んでみよう ☐
Practice 2 英語の強弱のリズムに注意して読んでみよう ☐
TRY! 1分20秒以内に本文全体を音読しよう ☐

Reading
本文の内容を読んで理解しよう【知識・技能】【思考力・判断力・表現力】

共通テスト GTEC®

Make the correct choice to complete each sentence or answer each question. (各5点)

(1) What does "contain" mean in line 5? ☐
　① divide　　　　② expose　　　　③ include　　　　④ keep

(2) Bananas are ☐.
　① believed to be bad for our health
　② eaten in many different ways around the world
　③ popular especially in Asian countries
　④ rich in vitamins but low in minerals

(3) Which of the following is true? ☐
　① A hot banana soup is made with some seasonings.
　② Bananas are in danger of extinction due to a lack of producers.
　③ Every culture has the same way of enjoying bananas.
　④ In Puerto Rico, sweet fried bananas are a common street food.

Vocabulary & Grammar　重要表現や文法事項について理解しよう【知識】　英検® GTEC®

Make the correct choice to complete each sentence. （各3点）

(1) The building is (　　　) danger of falling down.

① at ② in ③ on ④ with

(2) The organization is trying to save the penguins from (　　　).

① existence ② extinction ③ status ④ victim

(3) I was late for my appointment (　　　) to heavy traffic.

① according ② as ③ because ④ due

(4) His voice is familiar (　　　) radio listeners.

① at ② for ③ on ④ to

(5) Lack of money (　　　) to be a serious problem.

① feels ② looks ③ seems ④ sounds

🎧 Listening　英文を聞いて理解しよう【知識・技能】【思考力・判断力・表現力】　共通テスト　💿 8

Listen to the English and make the best choice to match the content. （4点）

① All types of bananas can be eaten raw.

② All types of bananas taste the same.

③ There are many different kinds of bananas all over the world.

💬 Interaction　英文を聞いて会話を続けよう【知識・技能】【思考力・判断力・表現力】　スピーキング・トレーナー　💿 9

Listen to the English and respond to the remark. （7点）

〔メ モ　　　　　　　　　　　　　　　　　　　　　　　　　　　　　　　　　　　　　　〕

🍌**Hints**
baked banana（焼きバナナ），banana cake（バナナケーキ），banana smoothie（バナナスムージー）

✍ Production（Writing）　自分の考えを書いて伝えよう【思考力・判断力・表現力】

Write your answer to the following question. （9点）

Explain how to cook your favorite dish.

🍌**Hints**
cut ... into bite-sized pieces（…を一口大に切る），fry（…を炒める），simmer（煮える），stir（[…を]かき混ぜる）

The future of bananas / is now at **risk** / due to Panama disease. // This disease **infects** banana plants / from their **roots** / and finally kills them. // It is caused / by a **specific** kind of **germ**. //

People once enjoyed a delicious kind of banana / named Gros Michel. // This
5 kind was produced / mainly in **Central** and South America. // In the 1950s, / however, / Panama disease attacked almost all the banana **plantations** there, / and Gros Michel nearly became **extinct**. // Instead, / people began / to produce another type of banana / called Cavendish. // It was **resistant** / to Panama disease. //

10 Again, / however, / a new type of Panama disease / began to infect bananas. // This disease is now **threatening** the production / of even Cavendish. // It is difficult / for modern technologies / to stop the disease. //

(122 words)

🔊 **音読しよう** 📖 ～～～～～～～～～ スピーキング・トレーナー

Practice 1 スラッシュ位置で文を区切って読んでみよう ☐
Practice 2 英語の強弱のリズムに注意して読んでみよう ☐
TRY! 1分35秒以内に本文全体を音読しよう ☐

📖 **Reading** 本文の内容を読んで理解しよう【知識・技能】【思考力・判断力・表現力】   共通テスト GTEC®

Make the correct choice to complete each sentence or answer each question.   (各5点[(3)は完答])

(1) What does "specific" mean in line 3? ☐
  ① common   ② correct   ③ particular   ④ usual

(2) ☐ nearly became extinct.
  ① Cavendish   ② Gros Michel
  ③ Both Cavendish and Gros Michel   ④ Panama disease

(3) Put the following events (①～④) into the order in which they happened.
  ☐ → ☐ → ☐ → ☐
  ① A new type of Panama disease began to attack bananas.
  ② Panama disease attacked Gros Michel.
  ③ People began to produce Cavendish.
  ④ People in Central and South America produced Gros Michel.

Vocabulary & Grammar　重要表現や文法事項について理解しよう【知識】　英検® GTEC®

Make the correct choice to complete each sentence.　(各3点)

(1) Exercise greatly reduces the (　　　) of heart disease.
　① difficulty　　　② disaster　　　③ method　　　④ risk

(2) Mosquitoes can (　　　) a great many people with malaria in this country.
　① convey　　　② deliver　　　③ expand　　　④ infect

(3) Tigers in India are (　　　) with extinction.
　① demanded　　　② suffered　　　③ requested　　　④ threatened

(4) Three people were (　　　) in that fire.
　① caused　　　② cheated　　　③ killed　　　④ released

(5) Would it be possible (　　　) me back tomorrow afternoon?
　① for you to call　　② of you to call　　③ for you calling　　④ of you calling

Listening　英文を聞いて理解しよう【知識・技能】【思考力・判断力・表現力】　共通テスト　🔘10

Listen to the English and make the best choice to match the content.　(4点)

① Bananas are a good source of energy during exercise.
② Japan imports bananas from overseas.
③ Many professional athletes like to eat bananas.

Interaction　英文を聞いて会話を続けよう【知識・技能】【思考力・判断力・表現力】　スピーキング・トレーナー　🔘11

Listen to the English and respond to the last remark.　(7点)

〔メモ 　　　　　　　　　　　　　　　　　　　　　　　　　　　　　　　　　〕

Hints
農業人口の高齢化に対する解決策を考えましょう。

Production (Writing)　自分の考えを書いて伝えよう【思考力・判断力・表現力】

Write your answer to the following question.　(9点)

Do you think farmers should grow fruits and vegetables without using chemicals? Why?

Hints
appearance (見た目), environment (環境), organic (有機栽培の), productivity (生産性)

Vivian: Why is it hard / to prevent Panama disease? //

Mr. Tanaka: Well, / one reason is / that most bananas / on the earth / have **identical genes**. // If one banana plant is infected / by a germ, / the **infection** can easily spread / to the rest / in the area. //

5　*Vivian:* Oh, / dear. //

Mr. Tanaka: **Besides** this, / the germs **exist** / in the ground. // They can move quickly / from one area / to another / through the **soil**. //

Vivian: Is there anything / we can do? //

Mr. Tanaka: Scientists are now trying / to find **effective** ways / to save

10　bananas. // One of the ways / is to **manipulate** the genes / of bananas. //

Vivian: I do hope / our **beloved** fruit will stay with us / forever! //

(102 words)

🔊 **音読しよう** 📖　　　　　　　　　　　スピーキング・トレーナー

Practice 1 スラッシュ位置で文を区切って読んでみよう ☐
Practice 2 英語の強弱のリズムに注意して読んでみよう ☐
TRY! 1分20秒以内に本文全体を音読しよう ☐

📖 Reading 本文の内容を読んで理解しよう【知識・技能】【思考力・判断力・表現力】　　共通テスト GTEC®

Make the correct choice to complete each sentence or answer each question. （各5点）

(1) What does "identical" mean in line 3? ☐
　① complex　　　② different　　　③ entire　　　④ same

(2) It is hard to prevent Panama disease. One of the reasons is that ☐.
　① bananas are produced in a specific region
　② studies on bananas haven't made much progress
　③ the germs can move quickly through the soil
　④ there are many different types of bananas

(3) Which of the following is true? ☐
　① All bananas on the earth have identical genes.
　② Bananas will stay with us forever.
　③ One way to save bananas from Panama disease is to manipulate their genes.
　④ We can do nothing to save bananas from Panama disease.

Vocabulary & Grammar 重要表現や文法事項について理解しよう【知識】 英検® GTEC®

Make the correct choice to complete each sentence. （各3点）

(1) Bad weather (　　　) us from arriving on time.

① avoided　　　　② held　　　　③ prevented　　　　④ stayed

(2) Companies (　　　) consumers to buy their products through advertising.

① damage　　　　② maintain　　　　③ manipulate　　　　④ predict

(3) The cancer (　　　) to other parts of his body.

① expected　　　　② raised　　　　③ protected　　　　④ spread

(4) Deep breathing is an (　　　) way to relieve stress.

① agricultural　　② effective　　　③ official　　　　④ uneasy

(5) I (　　　) my homework by myself.

① did did　　　　② did do　　　　③ do did　　　　④ do doing

Listening 英文を聞いて理解しよう【知識・技能】【思考力・判断力・表現力】 共通テスト 💿 12

Listen to the English and make the best choice to match the content. （4点）

① Japan imports a lot of bananas from the Philippines.

② Japan's self-sufficiency rate for bananas is about 80%.

③ The Philippines is the world's largest banana producer.

Interaction 英文を聞いて会話を続けよう【知識・技能】【思考力・判断力・表現力】 スピーキング・トレーナー 💿 13

Listen to the English and respond to the last remark. （7点）

〔メ モ　　　　　　　　　　　　　　　　　　　　　　　　　　　　　　　　　〕

🎧 **Hints**
I want to ~ のように文の形ではなく，農作物名だけを答えても構いません。

Production (Writing) 自分の考えを書いて伝えよう【思考力・判断力・表現力】

Write your answer to the following question. （9点）

Should genetically modified crops be banned? Why?

_____

_____

🎧 **Hints**
遺伝子組換え作物 (genetically modified crop) の是非について，自分の考えとその理由を書きましょう。

The graph shows / that the amount of **damage** / caused by natural disasters / increased year by year. // The **average** number of disasters / rose more than eight times / during a 30-year period. // According to the graph, / the number of **victims** rose **sharply** / in the period of 1987–1991 / and remained around 200

5 million. // The **cost** of damage also increased. // It reached well over 100 billion dollars / in the period of 2007–2011. //

Earthquakes, / **typhoons** / and **floods** / are becoming larger and larger / in **scale**. // Such natural disasters may hit us / **anytime**. // The damage can be much more severe / than you **expect**. // It is important / that you know / what

10 you will need / in case of a disaster. //

Thank you. //

(113 words)

音読しよう

スピーキング・トレーナー

Practice 1 スラッシュ位置で文を区切って読んでみよう ☐
Practice 2 英語の強弱のリズムに注意して読んでみよう ☐
TRY! 1分20秒以内に本文全体を音読しよう ☐

Reading 本文の内容を読んで理解しよう【知識・技能】【思考力・判断力・表現力】   共通テスト

Make the correct choice to answer each question. （各完答7点）

(1) Which of the following are true about the graph? (Choose two options. The order does not matter.) ☐ · ☐

① The amount of damage caused by natural disasters has decreased since 1997.

② The cost of damage was the largest between 2007 and 2011.

③ The cost of damage reached over 100 billion dollars for the first time in the period of 1987–1991.

④ The number of victims was the highest between 1987 and 1991.

⑤ The period of 2002–2006 had the highest number of natural disasters.

(2) Which of the following are true? (Choose two options. The order does not matter.) ☐ · ☐

① Earthquakes and floods are getting bigger and bigger in scale, but typhoons aren't.

② In most cases, the damage caused by natural disasters isn't as serious as we expect.

③ It is important for us to know what we'll need when a disaster happens.

④ Natural disasters can strike us anytime.

⑤ Natural disasters rarely occur around us.

Vocabulary & Grammar　重要表現や文法事項について理解しよう【知識】　英検® GTEC®

Make the correct choice to complete each sentence.　(各3点)

(1) The hurricane caused massive (　　　) to the city.
　① damage　　　　② experience　　　③ force　　　　④ recovery

(2) It was impossible to estimate the full (　　　) of the disaster.
　① depth　　　　② number　　　　③ scale　　　　④ shape

(3) I (　　　) to receive a call from Sam soon.
　① decide　　　　② expect　　　　③ predict　　　　④ think

(4) I'm carrying an umbrella (　　　) rain.
　① according to　　② in addition to　　③ in case of　　④ thanks to

(5) It is fortunate (　　　) you have such a good friend.
　① that　　　　　② to　　　　　③ which　　　　④ who

Listening　英文を聞いて理解しよう【知識・技能】【思考力・判断力・表現力】　共通テスト　🎧14

Listen to the English and make the best choice to match the content.　(5点)
　① Japan has solved the mechanism of how earthquakes occur.
　② Japan has suffered greatly from earthquakes.
　③ Japan is a country with many earthquakes.

Interaction　英文を聞いて会話を続けよう【知識・技能】【思考力・判断力・表現力】　スピーキング・トレーナー　🎧15

Listen to the English and respond to the last remark.　(7点)

〔メ　モ　　　　　　　　　　　　　　　　　　　　　　　　　　　　　　　　　　　　　　〕

🌡 **Hints**
　自然災害への備えとして実践していることを話しましょう。

Production (Writing)　自分の考えを書いて伝えよう【思考力・判断力・表現力】

Write your answer to the following question.　(9点)

What kind of measures do you think the government should take against natural disasters?

🌡 **Hints**
　政府は，自然災害に対してどのような取り組みをするべきでしょうか。

Typical natural disasters are different / from **region** to region. // Severe storms and floods often happen / in Asia. // In Central and South America, / huge earthquakes are likely to **occur**. // In Africa, / people **tend** to suffer / from terrible droughts. //

5　Japan has suffered / from earthquakes and typhoons / many times. // The Japanese government has collected data / about damage / caused by these disasters. // By using the data, / it has introduced various **measures** / to **avoid** **potential** risks / **related** to disasters / and has saved people's lives. //

One effective measure is / the use of hazard maps. // These maps show areas / 10　that can be affected / by floods and earthquakes. // They also tell people the **location** / of the nearest **evacuation** site / in each area. // The maps raise people's **awareness** / of **preventive** measures / against disasters. //

(124 words)

🔊)) **音読しよう** 〜〜〜〜〜〜〜〜〜〜〜〜〜〜〜〜〜〜〜〜〜〜〜〜　スピーキング・トレーナー

Practice 1 スラッシュ位置で文を区切って読んでみよう ☐
Practice 2 英語の強弱のリズムに注意して読んでみよう ☐
TRY! 1分30秒以内に本文全体を音読しよう ☐

📖 **Reading** 本文の内容を読んで理解しよう【知識・技能】【思考力・判断力・表現力】　共通テスト

Make the correct choice to complete each sentence. ((1)は7点. (2)は8点)

(1) You have learned that ☐.

① earthquakes and typhoons often happen in Japan

② huge earthquakes are likely to happen in Africa

③ severe storms and floods rarely happen in Asia

④ terrible droughts are likely to happen in Central and South America

(2) Hazard maps show us ☐.

① areas that can be affected by typhoons

② areas where floods and earthquakes happen

③ the time when natural disasters happen

④ where the nearest evacuation site is in each area

Vocabulary & Grammar   重要表現や文法事項について理解しよう【知識】   英検® GTEC®

Make the correct choice to complete each sentence.   (各3点)

(1) Women (　　　) to live longer than men.
　　① belong　　　　② offer　　　　③ rely　　　　④ tend

(2) We have to take (　　　) to reduce gas emissions.
　　① decisions　　② goals　　　　③ measures　　④ purposes

(3) The pilot changed course to (　　　) the storm.
　　① avoid　　　　② delay　　　　③ reduce　　　　④ visit

(4) Stress is related (　　　) poor sleep.
　　① as　　　　　② by　　　　　③ on　　　　　④ to

(5) He (　　　) sick in bed for a week when I visited him.
　　① is　　　　　② was　　　　③ has been　　④ had been

Listening   英文を聞いて理解しよう【知識・技能】【思考力・判断力・表現力】   共通テスト   💿16

Listen to the English and make the best choice to match the content.   (4点)

① The speaker used an elementary school as an evacuation site.

② The speaker was an elementary school teacher.

③ The speaker was in class at an elementary school when the typhoon hit.

Interaction   英文を聞いて会話を続けよう【知識・技能】【思考力・判断力・表現力】   スピーキング・トレーナー   💿17

Listen to the English and respond to the remark.   (7点)

〔メモ　　　　　　　　　　　　　　　　　　　　　　　　　　　　　　　　　　〕

🎧**Hints**
means of contact (連絡手段)，safety (安全)

Production (Writing)   自分の考えを書いて伝えよう【思考力・判断力・表現力】

Write your answer to the following question.   (9点)

Do you think hazard maps are useful? Why?

🎧**Hints**
本文第3段落の内容も参考にして書きましょう。

Preparing for Potential Risks

Once a natural disaster happens, / people **rush** to an evacuation site / like a school **gymnasium**. // Most people are not used to being with strangers / for a long time. // They experience **stress** / **arising** from the **loss** of privacy. //

Cardboard boxes have been used / to relieve such **discomfort**. // By using
5 them, / people are able to separate themselves / from others. // Also, / cardboard box beds are helpful / for keeping away the bitter cold / in gyms. //

Preventive measures against disasters / have **dramatically** improved our chances / of **surviving** them. // However, / it **depends** on each of us / to reduce our own risk / in future disasters. // It is never too early / to get **prepared** / for
10 them. //

(108 words)

🔊 **音読しよう** 📖 ～～～～～～ スピーキング・トレーナー

Practice 1 スラッシュ位置で文を区切って読んでみよう ☐
Practice 2 英語の強弱のリズムに注意して読んでみよう ☐
TRY! 1分15秒以内に本文全体を音読しよう ☐

📖 **Reading** 本文の内容を読んで理解しよう【知識・技能】【思考力・判断力・表現力】 共通テスト GTEC®

Make the correct choice to complete each sentence or answer each question. (各5点)

(1) What does "arise" mean in line 3? ☐
 ① arrive ② differ ③ happen ④ support

(2) Using cardboard boxes is useful for ☐.
 ① improving our chances of surviving disasters
 ② increasing our stress arising from the loss of privacy
 ③ keeping away the noise in an evacuation site
 ④ relieving the cold in an evacuation site

(3) Which of the following is true? ☐
 ① Cardboard boxes cannot be used as beds in an evacuation site.
 ② Natural disasters rarely happen, so there is no need to prepare for them.
 ③ Preventive measures against disasters have dramatically increased our risks.
 ④ We should get prepared for future disasters.

Vocabulary & Grammar　重要表現や文法事項について理解しよう【知識】　英検® GTEC®

Make the correct choice to complete each sentence.　(各3点)

(1) Maybe her headaches are caused by (　　　).
　　① pain　　　　　② patient　　　　③ spirit　　　　④ stress

(2) No one can (　　　) long without water.
　　① rescue　　　　② suffer　　　　③ survive　　　④ taste

(3) Your future (　　　) on what you do in the present.
　　① cooperates　　② depends　　　③ requires　　　④ treats

(4) I'm not used (　　　) treated like this.
　　① be　　　　　② being　　　　③ to be　　　　④ to being

(5) Have you ever (　　　) by a dog?
　　① bite　　　　　② bitten　　　　③ biting　　　　④ been bitten

Listening　英文を聞いて理解しよう【知識・技能】【思考力・判断力・表現力】　共通テスト 🔘18

Listen to the English and make the best choice to match the content.　(4点)

　　① A lot of natural disasters happen in Italy.

　　② In Italian shelters, people have to sleep on the ground.

　　③ Tents are set up at an evacuation site in Italy.

Interaction　英文を聞いて会話を続けよう【知識・技能】【思考力・判断力・表現力】　スピーキング・トレーナー 🔘19

Listen to the English and respond to the remark.　(7点)

〔メ モ　　　　　　　　　　　　　　　　　　　　　　　　　　　　　　　　　　　〕

🔔 **Hints**
避難所で生活する際に何があればよいか考えましょう。

Production (Writing)　自分の考えを書いて伝えよう【思考力・判断力・表現力】

Write your answer to the following question.　(9点)

What do you think is important when you stay at an evacuation site?

🔔 **Hints**
help each other (互いに助け合う), take care of one's health (健康管理をする)

International Festival / and Cultural Exchange //

August 1 @Room 101, / Daiichi Bldg. //

Come to Learn / about Your Neighbors! //

Schedule

5　10:00 – 10:10　Opening //

10:10 – 11:00　Japanese Cultural **Demonstrations** //

11:00 – 12:00　International Fashion Show / of Traditional **Clothing** //

12:00 – 14:00　Lunch **Buffet** / and Games //

14:00 – 15:00　**Workshop** / on How to Wear *Yukatas* //

10　15:00 – 15:10　**Closing** //

Come and join us. //　Everyone is welcome! //

For more information, / visit our website: / www.daiichi-ifce.org //

Admission is free //

Kumi: Hey, / there's going to be an international festival / on August 1. //　I'm

15　planning on going. //

David: Sounds good! //　In England / there are a lot of **immigrants** / now. //　In order to live / in **harmony** with each other, / I often went to international exchange events / there. //

Kumi: Oh, / I'm also interested / in these kinds of events. //　I'd like to study

20　abroad / next year. //

David: That's great! //

Kumi: Perhaps / foreign **residents** can tell me / what I need to do / before I go abroad. //

David: Good luck, / Kumi! //

(113 words)

🔊)) 【音読しよう】📖 ～～～～～～～～～～～～～～～～～ スピーキング・トレーナー

Practice 1　スラッシュ位置で文を区切って読んでみよう □

Practice 2　イントネーションに注意して読んでみよう □

TRY!　1分20秒以内に本文全体を音読しよう □

📖 **Reading**　本文の内容を読んで理解しよう【知識・技能】【思考力・判断力・表現力】　共通テスト GTEC®

Make the correct choice to answer each question.　((1)は 7 点, (2)は 8 点)

(1)　What does "international" mean in line 1?　□

①　domestic　　　　②　global　　　　③　local　　　　④　wild

(2)　Which of the following is true?　□

①　Kumi is going to organize an international festival.

②　Kumi is going to an international festival to make foreign friends.

③　Kumi wants to go to England to study English next year.

④　David took part in some international exchange events in England.

Vocabulary & Grammar 重要表現や文法事項について理解しよう【知識】 (英検®) (GTEC®)

Make the correct choice to complete each sentence. （各3点）

(1) (　　　　) order to become a doctor, you have to finish medical school.
　① As　　　　　② By　　　　　③ For　　　　　④ In

(2) My uncle has lived in a suburb in harmony (　　　) nature since he retired from work.
　① from　　　　② into　　　　③ to　　　　　④ with

(3) Foreign currency (　　　) rates can change sharply.
　① change　　　② exchange　　③ presentation　　④ variation

(4) She always recommends this book to anyone who is interested (　　　) musicals.
　① as　　　　　② in　　　　　③ on　　　　　④ to

(5) He told (　　　) the car would be ready next Friday.
　① to us if　　② to us that　　③ that to us　　④ us that

Listening 英文を聞いて理解しよう【知識・技能】【思考力・判断力・表現力】 (共通テスト) 🔘 20

Listen to the English and make the best choice to match the content. （4点）

　① The speaker met an Australian at the event.
　② The speaker went to Australia last weekend.
　③ The speaker will go to the international exchange event.

Interaction 英文を聞いて会話を続けよう【知識・技能】【思考力・判断力・表現力】 (スピーキング・トレーナー) 🔘 21

Listen to the English and respond to the last remark. （7点）

〔メ モ 　　　　　　　　　　　　　　　　　　　　　　　　　　　　　　　　　　　　　　　〕

🔔**Hints**
I'd like to [I want to] ~ の表現を使って伝えましょう。

Production (Writing) 自分の考えを書いて伝えよう【思考力・判断力・表現力】

Write your answer to the following question. （9点）

What kind of Japanese culture would you like to introduce to people from abroad?

_____

_____

🔔**Hints**
Japanese food (日本食), *kimono* (着物), manga (漫画), tea ceremony (茶道)

Lesson 4
To Make a More Open Society

Japan has become **internationalized**. // People from abroad / enjoy sightseeing / all over the country. // We also see foreign people / who are studying / and working / here and there. //

At convenience stores / in Japan, / people from other countries / serve as **cashiers politely** / and with smiles. // In **welfare facilities**, / care workers / from abroad / **devote** themselves / to helping elderly people. // They are welcomed / by the elderly / because they are kind and friendly / toward them. //

Another example is seen / in IT **industries**. // The number of people / from abroad / who work / as **advanced** engineers / and skilled **programmers** / is increasing. // They communicate well / with their Japanese **colleagues** / and do good work / in their companies. // Some of them **instruct** their **co-workers** / as **managers**. //

(114 words)

音読しよう

スピーキング・トレーナー

Practice 1 スラッシュ位置で文を区切って読んでみよう ☐
Practice 2 イントネーションに注意して読んでみよう ☐
TRY! 1分20秒以内に本文全体を音読しよう ☐

Reading 本文の内容を読んで理解しよう【知識・技能】【思考力・判断力・表現力】 共通テスト GTEC®

Make the correct choice to complete each sentence or answer each question. (各5点)

(1) In welfare facilities, people from other countries ☐.
  ① are welcomed by elderly people
  ② have difficulty in communicating with elderly people
  ③ instruct their co-workers as managers
  ④ serve as cashiers politely

(2) What does "advanced" mean in line 9? ☐
  ① bored   ② developed   ③ excited   ④ relaxed

(3) Which of the following is **not** true? ☐
  ① Many foreign people enjoy sightseeing all over Japan.
  ② Many Japanese people work in IT industries all over the world.
  ③ Several Japanese companies hire foreign workers.
  ④ There are some foreign students in Japan.

Vocabulary & Grammar　重要表現や文法事項について理解しよう【知識】　英検® GTEC®

Make the correct choice to complete each sentence.　(各3点)

(1) He devoted himself (　　　) writing mystery novels through his life.

　① as　　　　　② in　　　　　③ on　　　　　④ to

(2) A new nuclear power plant was built. The entire (　　　) cost hundreds of millions of dollars.

　① environment　② facility　　　③ industry　　　④ place

(3) She was promoted to sales (　　　) after only three years on the job.

　① customer　　② department　③ employer　　④ manager

(4) She (　　　) her child in using a computer.

　① consisted　　② insisted　　③ instructed　　④ served

(5) A child (　　　) parents are dead is called an orphan.

　① that　　　　② who　　　　③ whom　　　　④ whose

Listening　英文を聞いて理解しよう【知識・技能】【思考力・判断力・表現力】　共通テスト　22

Listen to the English and make the best choice to match the content.　(4点)

　① Some convenience stores employ foreign workers.

　② The speaker often goes shopping at a convenience store.

　③ The speaker works at a convenience store.

Interaction　英文を聞いて会話を続けよう【知識・技能】【思考力・判断力・表現力】　スピーキング・トレーナー　23

Listen to the English and respond to the last remark.　(7点)

〔メ モ　　　　　　　　　　　　　　　　　　　　　　　　　　　　　　　〕

▶Hints

shrine (神社), hot spring (温泉), temple (寺院), World Heritage Site (世界遺産)

Production (Writing)　自分の考えを書いて伝えよう【思考力・判断力・表現力】

Write your answer to the following question.　(9点)

What do you think is important when you work with people from other countries?

▶Hints

communication (コミュニケーション), conversation (会話), custom (習慣), value (価値)

Japan, / which has taken in a lot of foreign workers, / is getting some **benefits** / thanks to them. // **Nowadays**, / Japan's labor shortage is a **critical** problem. // People from abroad / have become an important **workforce**. // They will bring new ideas / and build good **atmospheres** / into **workplaces** / in Japan. //

5 There is another benefit. // Some Japanese companies / which employ foreign workers / make English an **official** language / at work. // The workers can share a wider **variety** of ideas. // As a result, / such companies are more likely to **succeed** / on the global stage. //

In order to make our society more open / to the world, / we need to make an 10 effort / to understand various ways of thinking / and respect different senses of **values**. // If we do this, / Japan will start a new **chapter** / so that we can all live better lives together. //

(135 words)

🔊)) **音読しよう** 📖 ～～～～～～～～～ **スピーキング・トレーナー**

Practice 1 スラッシュ位置で文を区切って読んでみよう ☐
Practice 2 イントネーションに注意して読んでみよう ☐
TRY! 1分35秒以内に本文全体を音読しよう ☐

📖 Reading 本文の内容を読んで理解しよう【知識・技能】【思考力・判断力・表現力】 共通テスト GTEC®

Make the correct choice to complete each sentence or answer each question. (各5点)

(1) What does "benefit" mean in line 1? ☐
　① advantage　　② damage　　③ dream　　④ recovery

(2) Which of the following is **not** a benefit that foreign workers can bring to Japan? ☐
　① Bringing new ideas into workplaces.
　② Becoming an important workforce.
　③ Being able to live better lives.
　④ For some companies, using English as an official language and succeeding internationally.

(3) If we try to understand various ways of thinking and respect different senses of values, ☐.
　① we can get a job abroad
　② we can have a more open society
　③ we can improve our English
　④ we can solve Japan's labor shortage

🎴 Vocabulary & Grammar 重要表現や文法事項について理解しよう【知識】 英検® GTEC®

Make the correct choice to complete each sentence. （各3点）

(1) This restaurant has a great (　　　).
　　① air　　　　　　　② atmosphere　　　③ cloud　　　　　④ sky

(2) Our classmates have a variety (　　　) different backgrounds.
　　① as　　　　　　　② from　　　　　　③ of　　　　　　　④ till

(3) He (　　　) in developing a new material.
　　① considered　　　② forgot　　　　　③ improved　　　④ succeeded

(4) I'd like to know the true (　　　) of this necklace.
　　① harmony　　　　② result　　　　　③ value　　　　　④ weapon

(5) My boss expects me to do the job in an hour, (　　　) is impossible.
　　① that　　　　　　② this　　　　　　③ what　　　　　④ which

🎧 Listening 英文を聞いて理解しよう【知識・技能】【思考力・判断力・表現力】 共通テスト 💿24

Listen to the English and make the best choice to match the content. （4点）
　① Chinese people are hardworking.
　② It is said that Chinese people like Japan.
　③ Many Chinese work in Japan.

💬 Interaction 英文を聞いて会話を続けよう【知識・技能】【思考力・判断力・表現力】 スピーキング・トレーナー 💿25

Listen to the English and respond to the last remark. （7点）
　〔メモ　　　　　　　　　　　　　　　　　　　　　　　　　　　　　　　　　〕

👆**Hints**
英語を社内公用語にするメリットとデメリットを考えましょう。

💬 Production (Speaking) 自分の考えを話して伝えよう【思考力・判断力・表現力】 スピーキング・トレーナー

Answer the following question. （9点）
Do you think Japanese companies should hire more foreign workers? Why?
　〔メモ　　　　　　　　　　　　　　　　　　　　　　　　　　　　　　　　　〕

👆**Hints**
外国人労働者を雇うメリット・デメリットを考えて話しましょう。

True Love between a Cat and a Dog

Our Recommended Book / for This Month: /

Coo and Shino //

On November 7, 2012, / the **kitten** was picked up / and taken home / by Haru-san. // She named him Coo. // Haru-san also looked after an old **female** dog, / Shino. //

5 When Coo and Shino saw each other / for the first time, / Coo seemed to fall in love / with her. // This was just the beginning / of their story. // Read a review / from one of our readers. //

David

A special **bond** / between a **feline** / named Coo / and his best **canine** friend, / Shino //

10 Cats and dogs are people's favorite pet animals. // Some people love dogs / because they are **loyal** / to their owners, / while others **appreciate** / that cats love living **independent** lives / on their own. // Well, / after you read this book, / you may come to **adore** both cats and dogs! //

(132 words)

🔊 **音読しよう** 📖 ～～～～～～～～～～～～～～～～～～～～ スピーキング・トレーナー

Practice 1 スラッシュ位置で文を区切って読んでみよう ☐
Practice 2 イントネーションに注意して読んでみよう ☐
TRY! 1分30秒以内に本文全体を音読しよう ☐

📖 **Reading** 本文の内容を読んで理解しよう【知識・技能】【思考力・判断力・表現力】　　共通テスト GTEC®

Make the correct choice to complete each sentence or answer each question. （各5点）

(1) What does "look after" mean in line 4? ☐
　　① belong to　　　　② look for　　　　③ take care of　　　④ take part in

(2) On November 7, 2012, ☐.
　　① David picked up a cat and named him Coo
　　② David picked up a dog and named her Shino
　　③ Haru-san picked up a cat and named him Coo
　　④ Haru-san picked up a dog and named her Shino

(3) According to David's review, ☐.
　　① cats love living independent lives on their own, so they're not popular as pets
　　② dogs are loyal to their owners
　　③ dogs are the most popular as pets
　　④ people prefer cats to dogs

🗂 Vocabulary & Grammar　重要表現や文法事項について理解しよう【知識】　英検® GTEC®

Make the correct choice to complete each sentence.　（各3点）

(1) If you go to New York, I (　　　) visiting the Metropolitan Museum.
　① explain　　　　② offer　　　　　③ recommend　　　④ try

(2) Our classmates formed strong (　　　) with each other.
　① bonds　　　　② bones　　　　　③ cells　　　　　④ objects

(3) He is (　　　) from his parents but still asks for their advice.
　① confident　　② independent　　③ loyal　　　　④ particular

(4) I picked (　　　) the pen from the floor.
　① by　　　　　② for　　　　　　③ to　　　　　　④ up

(5) The children were (　　　) their aunt.
　① brought　　　② brought by　　　③ brought up　　④ brought up by

🎧 Listening　英文を聞いて理解しよう【知識・技能】【思考力・判断力・表現力】　共通テスト 💿26

Listen to the English and make the best choice to match the content.　（4点）
　① The speaker hardly takes care of her dog.
　② The speaker has a dog.
　③ The speaker wants to have a pet.

💬 Interaction　英文を聞いて会話を続けよう【知識・技能】【思考力・判断力・表現力】　スピーキング・トレーナー 💿27

Listen to the English and respond to the last remark.　（7点）
〔メモ　　　　　　　　　　　　　　　　　　　　　　　　　　　　　　　　　　　　　　　〕

🎤 **Hints**
My favorite book is ... や I like ... などの表現を使って話しましょう。

✍ Production (Writing)　自分の考えを書いて伝えよう【思考力・判断力・表現力】

Write your answer to the following question.　（9点）
Which do you want to have as a pet, cats or dogs?　Why?

🎤 **Hints**
bark（吠える），friendly（人懐っこい），loyal（忠実な），smart（賢い），take ... for a walk（…を散歩に連れて行く）

Lesson 5

True Love between a Cat and a Dog

I tried everything / to attract Shino's attention. // Softly and **gently**, / I **stretched** out my **paw** / to her. // As soon as I touched her, / however, / Shino stood up / and left me all alone. // Still, / I never gave up. //

Day after day, / I stayed beside Shino / and followed her / to every corner of
5 Haru-san's home. // Then, / one day, / Shino reached out her paw, / and I softly touched it. // Finally, / **mutual** trust was being built / between us. //

Shino often spent the day / sitting in the sun / near the window. // We sometimes played **hide-and-seek** / under a *kotatsu*. // Every day, / Haru-san took us for walks / in the **neighborhood**. // When we **bumped** into another dog / we
10 knew, / we got excited. //

It seemed like **serene** and happy days / like this / would last forever. //

(126 words)

音読しよう 📖

━━━━━━━━━━━━━━━━━━━━━━━━━━━━━━━━━━ スピーキング・トレーナー

Practice 1 スラッシュ位置で文を区切って読んでみよう ☐
Practice 2 イントネーションに注意して読んでみよう ☐
TRY! 1分30秒以内に本文全体を音読しよう ☐

📖 Reading 本文の内容を読んで理解しよう【知識・技能】【思考力・判断力・表現力】   共通テスト

Make the correct choice to complete each sentence or answer each question.   ((1)は7点, (2)は8点)

(1) ☐ are two things Coo did to attract Shino's attention.

A : follow her to every corner of the house

B : play hide-and-seek

C : sit in the sun near the window

D : stay close to her

E : stroke her body

① A and B   ② A and D

③ B and D   ④ C and E

⑤ D and E

(2) Which of the following is true? ☐

① Coo and Shino finally became friends.

② Coo and Shino played hide-and-seek in the yard.

③ Coo gave up becoming friends with Shino.

④ When Coo and Shino came across another dog, they were frightened and ran away.

🏷 Vocabulary & Grammar　重要表現や文法事項について理解しよう【知識】　英検®　GTEC®

Make the correct choice to complete each sentence.　(各3点)

(1) I (　　　) across the table to reach the salt.

① covered　　　② extended　　　③ stayed　　　④ stretched

(2) I'll do my homework (　　　) this TV program is over.

① as if　　　② as soon as　　　③ even if　　　④ every time

(3) I've given (　　　) trying to persuade him into changing his mind.

① away　　　② in　　　③ off　　　④ up

(4) We spent the evening (　　　) about our vacation.

① talk　　　② talked　　　③ talking　　　④ to talk

(5) A railway bridge is already (　　　) over the river.

① been building　　　② been built　　　③ being built　　　④ building

🎧 Listening　英文を聞いて理解しよう【知識・技能】【思考力・判断力・表現力】　共通テスト　⊙ 28

Listen to the English and make the best choice to match the content.　(4点)

① The speaker has known Kate since last year.

② The speaker organized the party last year.

③ The speaker went to the party, but Kate didn't.

💬 Interaction　英文を聞いて会話を続けよう【知識・技能】【思考力・判断力・表現力】　スピーキング・トレーナー　⊙ 29

Listen to the English and respond to the remark.　(7点)

〔メ モ　　　　　　　　　　　　　　　　　　　　　　　　　　　　　　　　　　〕

🌡 **Hints**

get good grades(よい成績を収める)，spend time with family members(家族と過ごす)，talk with a friend(友達と話す)

😃 Production (Speaking)　自分の考えを話して伝えよう【思考力・判断力・表現力】　スピーキング・トレーナー

Answer the following question.　(9点)

Introduce one of your best friends.

〔メ モ　　　　　　　　　　　　　　　　　　　　　　　　　　　　　　　　　　〕

🌡 **Hints**

親友との出会い，親友の性格などについて話しましょう。

Lesson 5 True Love between a Cat and a Dog

Then, / one day / in 2014, / Shino began to walk straight into walls / and even got herself **stuck** / in small spaces. //　Soon, / she started to circle / around the same place / again and again. //　Later, / Shino was **diagnosed** / with **dementia**. //

I decided to do everything / I could for Shino. //　When she got lost, / I served 5 as her guide. //　Shino seemed to feel comfortable / when she placed her head / on my back. //　**Despite** all these efforts, / however, / in the summer of 2017, / Shino couldn't stand up / at all. //

One night, / Shino started to **bark** out **violently**. //　I didn't know the reason / why she was **howling** so hard. //　Early the next morning, / Shino was taken / to 10 a **veterinarian nearby** / and was **hospitalized**. //

(118 words)

)) 音読しよう

Practice 1 スラッシュ位置で文を区切って読んでみよう ☐
Practice 2 イントネーションに注意して読んでみよう ☐
TRY! 1分20秒以内に本文全体を音読しよう ☐

スピーキング・トレーナー

Reading　本文の内容を読んで理解しよう【知識・技能】【思考力・判断力・表現力】　　共通テスト GTEC®

Make the correct choice to complete each sentence or answer each question.　(各5点)

(1)　What does "serve" mean in line 4?　☐
　　　① achieve　　　　② consume　　　　③ realize　　　　④ work

(2)　You have learned that Coo ☐.
　　　① circled around the same place again and again
　　　② let Shino put her head on his back
　　　③ slept next to Shino every night
　　　④ walked straight into walls

(3)　What happened in the summer of 2017?　☐
　　　① Coo got lost during a walk.
　　　② Coo was hospitalized.
　　　③ Shino was diagnosed with dementia.
　　　④ Shino was unable to stand up at all.

🏷️ Vocabulary & Grammar　重要表現や文法事項について理解しよう【知識】　英検® GTEC®

Make the correct choice to complete each sentence.　（各3点）

(1) I couldn't sleep well last night because the dog was (　　　) all night.
　① barking　　　② singing　　　③ treating　　　④ whispering

(2) Though it was late, we decided (　　　) our friends.
　① visit　　　② visiting　　　③ to visit　　　④ to visiting

(3) We enjoyed the trip (　　　) the bad weather.
　① although　　　② because　　　③ despite　　　④ until

(4) She made an (　　　) to master English.
　① ability　　　② attitude　　　③ effort　　　④ intelligence

(5) This is (　　　) we came to know each other.
　① how　　　② that　　　③ the way how　　　④ which

🎧 Listening　英文を聞いて理解しよう【知識・技能】【思考力・判断力・表現力】　共通テスト　💿 30

Listen to the English and make the best choice to match the content.　（4点）

　① The speaker has had a cat for a long time.
　② The speaker often fights with her cat.
　③ The speaker was encouraged by her cat when she was depressed.

💬 Interaction　英文を聞いて会話を続けよう【知識・技能】【思考力・判断力・表現力】　スピーキング・トレーナー　💿 31

Listen to the English and respond to the last remark.　（7点）

　〔メ モ　　　　　　　　　　　　　　　　　　　　　　　　　　　　　　　　　〕

🖐 **Hints**
　activate communication（コミュニケーションを活性化する），animal therapy（アニマルセラピー），heal（…を癒やす）

✒️ Production（Writing）　自分の考えを書いて伝えよう【思考力・判断力・表現力】

Write your answer to the following question.　（9点）

Imagine you were Coo. What did you tell Shino when she was hospitalized?

🖐 **Hints**
　くぅの気持ちを想像してみましょう。

At 2:30 p.m. / on the day / when Shino was hospitalized, / there was a call / from the hospital, / and the vet said, / "Shino-chan's heart has stopped." // When Haru-san arrived at the hospital, / the doctor was still **attempting** / to **revive** Shino. // After **approximately** ten minutes, / Haru-san said / to the vet, / "That is
5 enough. // Shino has **comforted** us so much." // Shino finally stopped breathing / in peace. //

After Shino left us, / Haru-san talked to me gently / and **embraced** me warmly. // But I didn't feel like talking / to anybody. // I didn't even have an **appetite**. //

As time went by, / however, / my **sorrow** gradually **lessened**. // I came to
10 think / that Shino would always watch over us / with her gentle eyes. // In our yard, / where Shino and I had spent so much time together, / the cherry blossoms were in full **bloom**. //

(134 words)

🔊)) 【音読しよう】 ～～～～～～～～～～～～～～～～ 【スピーキング・トレーナー】

Practice 1 スラッシュ位置で文を区切って読んでみよう ☐
Practice 2 イントネーションに注意して読んでみよう ☐
TRY! 1分30秒以内に本文全体を音読しよう ☐

📖 **Reading** 本文の内容を読んで理解しよう【知識・技能】【思考力・判断力・表現力】   共通テスト GTEC®

Make the correct choice to complete each sentence or answer each question. (各5点)

(1) What does "attempt" mean in line 3? ☐
   ① encourage   ② provide   ③ support   ④ try

(2) At the hospital, ☐.
   ① Haru-san asked the doctor to revive Shino
   ② Haru-san didn't wish to extend Shino's life
   ③ Haru-san embraced Coo and that helped him get through his sorrow
   ④ the doctor brought Shino back to life

(3) Which of the following is true? ☐
   ① Coo gradually got over his sorrow of losing Shino.
   ② Coo thinks that Shino's spirit is not with him.
   ③ Haru-san planted a cherry tree in her yard.
   ④ When Shino died, the cherry blossoms in the yard were in full bloom.

🏷️ Vocabulary & Grammar　重要表現や文法事項について理解しよう【知識】　英検® GTEC®

Make the correct choice to complete each sentence. （各3点）

(1) Words may not be enough for (　　　　) you when you are in great sorrow.
　① arranging　　　② comforting　　　③ discussing　　　④ pushing

(2) Mary expressed her (　　　　) at her father's death.
　① communication　② judgement　　　③ memory　　　　④ sorrow

(3) This evening I (　　　　) like going to a movie.
　① do　　　　　　② feel　　　　　　③ wish　　　　　④ would

(4) Regular exercise (　　　　) the chance of heart disease.
　① hides　　　　　② lessens　　　　③ requires　　　④ treats

(5) He went to Boston, (　　　　) he met his uncle.
　① how　　　　　② when　　　　　③ where　　　④ which

🎧 Listening　英文を聞いて理解しよう【知識・技能】【思考力・判断力・表現力】　共通テスト　32

Listen to the English and make the best choice to match the content. （4点）

　① The speaker failed the test.
　② The speaker is going to take the examination.
　③ The speaker is happy that she passed the examination.

💬 Interaction　英文を聞いて会話を続けよう【知識・技能】【思考力・判断力・表現力】　スピーキング・トレーナー　33

Listen to the English and respond to the last remark. （7点）

〔メ モ　　　　　　　　　　　　　　　　　　　　　　　　　　　　　　　〕

🔔 Hints
engineer (エンジニア), firefighter (消防士), hairstylist (美容師), kindergarten teacher (幼稚園の先生),
office worker (会社員)

✏️ Production（Writing）　自分の考えを書いて伝えよう【思考力・判断力・表現力】

Write your answer to the following question. （9点）

How do you spend your time when you are feeling down?

🔔 Hints
落ち込んだときの過ごし方について書きましょう。listen to ... (…を聞く)，talk with ... (…と話す)

It was a very happy **funeral**, / a great **success**. // Even the sun shone / that day / for the late Henry Ground. // Lying in his **coffin**, / he was probably enjoying himself / too. // Once more, / and for the last time / on this earth, / he was the center / of attention. // Yes, / it was a very happy **occasion**. // People laughed /
5 and told each other jokes. // **Relatives** / who had not spoken / for years / smiled at each other / and promised to stay in touch. // And, / of course, / everyone had a favorite story / to tell about Henry. //

"Do you remember the time / he dressed up / in very strange clothes / and went from door to door / telling people's **fortunes**? // He actually made six
10 **pounds** / in an afternoon!" //

"I was once having dinner / with him / in a restaurant. // When the wine waiter brought the wine, / he **poured** a drop / into Henry's glass / and waited / with a **superior expression** / on his face, / as if to say / 'Taste it. // It's clear / that you know *nothing* / about wine.' // So Henry, / instead of tasting it / the way /
15 any **normal** person would do, / put his **thumb** and **forefinger** / into the wine. // Then he put his hand to his ear / and **rubbed** his forefinger and thumb together / as if he were *listening* to the quality / of the wine! // Then he **nodded** / to the wine waiter seriously, / as if to say / 'Yes, / that's fine. // You may serve it.' // You should have seen the wine waiter's face! // I still don't know / how Henry
20 **managed** to keep a straight face!" //

"Old Henry loved / to pull people's legs. // Once, / when he was invited / to an **exhibition** / of some modern painter's **latest** work, / he managed **somehow** to get into the exhibition hall / the day before / and turn all the paintings **upside** down. // The exhibition ran / for four days / before anyone noticed / what he
25 had done!" //

"It's hard / to believe / that Henry was a Ground / when you think / how different he was from his brothers." //

(323 words)

Practice 1 スラッシュ位置で文を区切って読んでみよう ☐
Practice 2 イントネーションに注意して読んでみよう ☐
TRY! 3分30秒以内に本文全体を音読しよう ☐

スピーキング・トレーナー

Reading 本文の内容を読んで理解しよう【知識・技能】【思考力・判断力・表現力】

Make the correct choice to complete each sentence or answer each question. （各5点）

(1) Why was there a feeling of happiness at Henry's funeral? ☐

① Because everyone had a happy memory of Henry.

② Because everyone was the center of attention with their favorite jokes.

③ Because Henry was a person who caused a lot of trouble to people around him.

④ Because his friends got together after being apart for a long time.

(2) What did Henry do in very strange clothes? ☐

① He got into an exhibition hall and turned the paintings upside down.

② He made money by telling people's fortunes.

③ He put his thumb and forefinger into the wine.

④ He went to a restaurant.

(3) The phrase "keep a straight face" in line 20 means "☐."

① accept a difficult or unpleasant situation

② make an expression that shows that you do not like someone or something

③ prevent yourself from losing the respect of other people

④ stop yourself from smiling or laughing

Vocabulary 重要表現について理解しよう【知識】

Make the correct choice to complete each sentence. （各3点）

(1) Many people in the audience (　　　) in agreement.

① encountered　　② extended　　③ nodded　　④ prepared

(2) You can take the boat (　　　) driving around the lake.

① against　　② in favor of　　③ in spite of　　④ instead of

(3) It is quite (　　　) for people to be afraid of the dark.

① normal　　② perfect　　③ special　　④ unusual

(4) Ralph (　　　) his hands together to keep them warm.

① folded　　② raised　　③ rubbed　　④ shook

(5) The box was heavy, but she (　　　) to carry it to the car.

① failed　　② hesitated　　③ managed　　④ pretended

Yes, / it was difficult / to believe / that he was a Ground. // He was born / into an **unimportant** but **well-to-do** Midlands family. // He was the youngest / of five sons. // The Grounds were all handsome: / **blue-eyed**, / **fair-haired**, / clever / and **hardworking**. // The four older boys / all made a success of their lives. //

5 The eldest became a **clergyman**; / the second ended up / as the **headmaster** / of a famous public school; / the third went into business / and became very rich; / the fourth became a **lawyer** / like his father. // That is why everybody was surprised / when the youngest Ground, Henry, / turned out to be a **good-for-nothing.** //

10 Unlike his brothers, / he had brown eyes and dark hair, / but was as handsome and **charming** / as the rest, / which made him quite a **lady-killer**. // And, / although he never married, / there is no **doubt** at all / that Henry Ground loved women. // He also loved eating, / drinking, / laughing, / talking, / and a thousand other activities / which don't make money / or improve the human **condition**. //

15 One of his favorite ways / of spending time / was doing nothing. // His idea of an **energetic** afternoon / when the sun was shining / was to sit / in the **shade** of a tree, / with a pretty **companion** / by his side, / talking of this and that, / **counting** the **blades** of grass, / and learning the songs of the birds. //

(217 words)

 音読しよう スピーキング・トレーナー

Practice 1 スラッシュ位置で文を区切って読んでみよう ☐
Practice 2 イントネーションに注意して読んでみよう ☐
TRY! 2分20秒以内に本文全体を音読しよう ☐

Make the correct choice to answer each question. （(1)は 7 点，(2)は完答 8 点）

(1) Which of the following is **not** true? ☐

① Henry was not as clever or hardworking as his brothers, so everybody knew that he would not make a success of his life.

② Henry's brothers all made a success of their own lives.

③ Henry's father was a lawyer.

④ Unlike his brothers, Henry was a good-for-nothing.

(2) Which of the following are true? (Choose two options. The order does not matter.)

☐ · ☐

① Henry and his brothers were handsome and charming. They were all quite the lady-killers.

② Henry looked like his brothers. He also had brown eyes and dark hair.

③ Henry remained single all his life, but he enjoyed friendly relations with women.

④ Henry was interested in many things and led a very active and energetic life.

⑤ Henry was interested in making money and improving people's lives.

⑥ On pleasant afternoons, Henry was seen sitting with a pretty woman in the shade of a tree.

Make the correct choice to complete each sentence. （各 3 点）

(1) She had always wanted to be a writer but (   ) up as a teacher.

   ① came   ② ended   ③ kept   ④ showed

(2) It rained this morning, but it (   ) out to be a lovely day.

   ① changed   ② set   ③ showed   ④ turned

(3) (   ) beef, chicken has very little fat.

   ① According to   ② In exchange for   ③ Instead   ④ Unlike

(4) He says he can do it, but I still have my (   ) about his ability.

   ① challenges   ② doubts   ③ opinions   ④ questions

(5) The sun was hot, and there were no trees to offer us (   ).

   ① protection   ② rest   ③ shade   ④ water

Anyway, / the stories went on / even while the coffin was being lowered / into the **grave**. // People held **handkerchiefs** to their eyes, / but their tears were tears of laughter, / not sadness. // Later, / there was a funeral breakfast, / by **invitation** only. // It was attended / by twelve of Henry's closest friends. //

5 Henry Ground had asked his brother, / Colin, / to read out his will / during the funeral breakfast. // Everyone was curious / about Henry Ground's will. // Henry had always been borrowing money / from others, / hadn't he? // What could he **possibly** have to leave / in a will? //

Colin cleared his **throat**. // "Ahem! // If you are ready, / ladies and gentlemen." //
10 Everyone **settled** down, / **anxious** to know / what was in the will. // Colin opened the will. // When he **announced** / that Henry Ground was, / in fact, / **worth** at least three-quarters of a million pounds, / everyone **gasped**. // But who was going to get it? // Eyes **narrowed** / and throats went dry. //

"You are all such dear friends of mine," / Colin went on, / "that I cannot decide /
15 which of you to leave my money to." // Colin **paused**. // In the silence, / you could have heard a **pin** drop. // He began to read the will / again. // "So, / dear friends, / I have set you a little competition. // Each of you / in turn / must tell the funniest joke / he or she can think of, / and the one / who gets the most laughter / will get my fortune. // Colin will be the only judge / of the best
20 joke." //

(240 words)

Practice 1 スラッシュ位置で文を区切って読んでみよう ☐
Practice 2 イントネーションに注意して読んでみよう ☐
TRY! 2分30秒以内に本文全体を音読しよう ☐

スピーキング・トレーナー

📖 Reading

本文の内容を読んで理解しよう【知識・技能】【思考力・判断力・表現力】 〔共通テスト〕

Make the correct choice to answer each question. ((1)は完答 7 点, (2)は完答 8 点)

(1) Which of the following are **not** true? (Choose two options. The order does not matter.) □ · □

① After Henry's funeral, a funeral breakfast was served for his friends.

② Henry left over three-quarters of a million pounds in his will.

③ Henry's brother, Colin, read his will during the funeral breakfast.

④ Henry's friends expected that they would talk about their shares of his fortune.

⑤ There was a feeling of happiness in the air throughout Henry's funeral.

⑥ Three-quarters of a million pounds were not so large an amount of money in those days.

(2) Which of the following are true? (Choose two options. The order does not matter.) □ · □

① Henry had decided which of his friends to leave his money to, but he couldn't announce it.

② Henry had set a little competition to decide who was going to get his money.

③ Henry's money was to be given to the person whose joke got the most laughter from Colin.

④ It was not his friends but Colin that would judge whose joke got the most laughter.

⑤ The silence was broken by a pin which fell by accident.

🎴 Vocabulary

重要表現について理解しよう【知識】 〔英検®〕〔GTEC®〕

Make the correct choice to complete each sentence. (各 3 点)

(1) She ( ) in surprise when she heard the news.
　① blew　　　② breathed　　　③ gasped　　　④ sighed

(2) America is ( ) that it has several time zones.
　① so a big country　　　　　② such a big country
　③ too big a country　　　　　④ very big a country

(3) He ( ) to take a drink of water and then continued speaking.
　① coughed　　② finished　　③ nodded　　④ paused

(4) Each of us read the magazine ( ) turn.
　① by　　　② in　　　③ to　　　④ with

(5) I entered the painting ( ) and won first prize.
　① competition　　② event　　③ exhibition　　④ program

The first person stood up / and told a very funny joke / about an Englishman / who fell in love / with his umbrella. // When he finished, / he was in tears of laughter, / for he always laughed / at his own jokes. // The rest of the company / remained *completely silent.* // You could tell / from their red faces / that they

5　found the joke funny, / but not one of them wanted to laugh, / and give him the chance / to win the competition. // The second told a story / about a hungry pig, / which was so good that, / some years later, / a movie company paid for the story. // When she sat down, / the others **buried** their faces / in their handkerchiefs, / pretended to **sneeze**, / dropped pencils / under the table /

10　—— anything to cover up their laughter. // And so / it went on, / joke after wonderful joke, / the **sort** of jokes / that would make your sides **ache**. // And yet, / everybody somehow kept from laughing! //

By the time / the last joke had been told, / every one of the twelve / was sitting perfectly still, / **desperately** holding in the laughter / which was bursting

15　to get out. // Their **desire** to laugh / had built up such a pressure: / it was like a **volcano** / ready to **erupt**. //

Silence. // **Painful** silence. //

Suddenly, / Colin sneezed. // A perfectly ordinary sneeze. // Atishoo. // Then / he took out a **ridiculously** large handkerchief / with red spots on it / and blew

20　his nose. // Bbbrrrrrrppp. //

That was enough. // Someone burst out laughing, / **unable** to hold it in any longer. // That started the others off. // In no time, / everyone **bent** over, / tears running down their **cheeks** / as they laughed. // Of course, / they were not just laughing / at the sneeze, / **nor** even at the twelve jokes. // No, / they were

25　laughing / at themselves / as they realized / that Henry Ground had led them / into his last, and funniest, **practical** joke, / setting their need to laugh / against their **greed** for money. //

(309 words)

Practice 1 スラッシュ位置で文を区切って読んでみよう ☐
Practice 2 イントネーションに注意して読んでみよう ☐
TRY! 3分20秒以内に本文全体を音読しよう ☐

スピーキング・トレーナー

Make the correct choice to complete each sentence or answer each question. （各5点）

(1) Each of the guests told his or her funniest joke in turn, but all the others didn't laugh.　Why not? ☐
   ① Because each of them believed his or her own joke was better than the others' jokes.
   ② Because none of their jokes were so funny for the listeners.
   ③ Because their laughter would give the joker the chance to win the competition.
   ④ Because they knew that it was bad manners to laugh at the table of a funeral breakfast.

(2) The phrase "hold in the laughter" in line 14 is closest in meaning to "☐."
   ① burst into laughter
   ② have a good laugh
   ③ make someone else laugh
   ④ stop yourself from laughing

(3) When all of the guests burst out laughing, they realized that ☐.
   ① Colin had also been deceived by Henry
   ② Colin had won the competition
   ③ Henry had not left any money to anyone
   ④ it had all been Henry's practical joke

Make the correct choice to complete each sentence. （各3点）

(1) She (　　　) her face in her hands and began to cry.
   ① buried　　　　② covered　　　　③ pressed　　　　④ turned

(2) His family tried to (　　　) up the real cause of his death.
   ① cover　　　　② give　　　　③ keep　　　　④ make

(3) The old lady had a burning (　　　) to go back to her home country before she died.
   ① chance　　　　② desire　　　　③ duty　　　　④ reason

(4) The children (　　　) up their balloons and threw them into the air.
   ① blew　　　　② burned　　　　③ burst　　　　④ flew

(5) Tom was (　　　) to go to work today because he was ill.
   ① about　　　　② belong　　　　③ ready　　　　④ unable

When, / at long last, / the laughter had died down, / Colin cleared his throat / once more. // **"Forgive** my little piece of theater," / he said, / his eyes **twinkling**. // "I have been practicing that sneeze / for a week or more." // He folded the large handkerchief / and put it back / into his pocket. // "Henry's idea, / of course," /

5 he added, / **unnecessarily**. // All twelve guests realized / they had been set up beautifully. //

"Ahem! // May I read you the rest of the will / now?" // Colin asked. //

"My friends," / the last part of Henry's will / began, / "forgive me, / but I couldn't help playing one last little joke / on you. // It's good / to know / that

10 your love of laughter / finally **overcame** your love of money." //

Colin paused, / letting the meaning of the words / come home to everybody. // Then / he read out the final part / of the late Henry Ground's last will. //

"My friends, / thank you for letting me / have the last laugh. // As for the money: / because I love you all, / my fortune will be **divided equally** / among you. //

15 Enjoy your share, / and think of me / **whenever** you hear laughter." //

The company fell silent. // For the first time / that day, / there was a feeling of sadness / in the air. //

(200 words)

音読しよう))) ・・・・・・・・・・・・・・・・・・・・・ スピーキング・トレーナー

Practice 1 スラッシュ位置で文を区切って読んでみよう ☐
Practice 2 イントネーションに注意して読んでみよう ☐
TRY! 2分10秒以内に本文全体を音読しよう ☐

Reading 本文の内容を読んで理解しよう【知識・技能】【思考力・判断力・表現力】 共通テスト GTEC®

Make the correct choice to complete each sentence or answer each question. ((1)は7点,(2)は8点)

(1) The sentence "they had been set up" in line 5 is closest in meaning to "[   ]."

   ① they had been laughed at for being very foolish

   ② they had been led into Henry's practical joke

   ③ they had proved themselves to be Henry's good friends

   ④ they had recognized that Henry's will was a false one

(2) What did Henry think would happen? [   ]

   ① He thought that his friends would overcome their love of laughter.

   ② He thought that his friends would overcome their love of money.

   ③ He thought that his money would awaken a new love of money in his friends.

   ④ He thought that his money would develop a new love of laughter in his friends.

Vocabulary 重要表現について理解しよう【知識】 英検® GTEC®

Make the correct choice to complete each sentence. (各3点)

(1) She said that she would be late and (   ) that she was sorry.

   ① added   ② agreed   ③ explained   ④ insisted

(2) We are having (   ) at our house for dinner today.

   ① customers   ② guests   ③ passengers   ④ tourists

(3) He looked so funny that I couldn't (   ) laughing.

   ① deny   ② help   ③ stay   ④ try

(4) It has taken me a while, but at last I've (   ) my fear of public speaking.

   ① overcome   ② overflowed   ③ overtaken   ④ overworked

(5) Tom is in his room. (   ) Steve, I have no idea where he is.

   ① According to   ② As for   ③ In addition to   ④ Thanks to

A Society with Drones

Vivian: Hey, / what are you watching? //

Takashi: I'm watching soccer! //

Vivian: That's soccer? // Those look like **drones**, / not soccer balls! //

Takashi: That's right. // Five players / on each team / are trying to score goals /

5   with drones. // A goal is scored / when a drone goes through the ring. // The team / with more points / wins. //

Vivian: Playing drone soccer / looks more difficult / than playing soccer / on a field! //

Takashi: It really is. // Players need excellent skills / because the ring is only 55 centimeters / in diameter. //

10 *Vivian:* I see. // Oh, / the players are flying the drones / at **extremely** high speeds! //

Takashi: Right. // I saw a news story / about a drone race / the other day. // I was surprised / that an eleven-year-old boy won the race! //

Vivian: Fantastic! //

15 *Takashi:* New technologies are creating new forms of **entertainment** / and making them more **enjoyable**. //

(126 words)

音読しよう

スピーキング・トレーナー

Practice 1 スラッシュ位置で文を区切って読んでみよう ☐

Practice 2 イントネーションに注意して読んでみよう ☐

TRY! 1分20秒以内に本文全体を音読しよう ☐

Reading 本文の内容を読んで理解しよう【知識・技能】【思考力・判断力・表現力】 共通テスト

Make the correct choice to complete each sentence or answer each question. (各5点)

(1) Takashi is watching ☐.

  ① a drone race   ② a drone soccer game

  ③ a soccer game with 22 players   ④ a TV program about drones

(2) Takashi thinks that playing drone soccer ☐.

  ① is as difficult as playing soccer on a field

  ② is easier than playing soccer on a field

  ③ is more difficult than playing soccer on a field

  ④ requires fewer skills than playing soccer on a field

(3) Which of the following is true for drone soccer rules? ☐

  ① Eleven players on each team play a soccer game.

  ② Players fly their drones at moderate speeds during the game.

  ③ The goal ring is as big as a soccer ball used on a field.

  ④ When the player passes the drone through the ring, a goal is scored.

Vocabulary & Grammar　重要表現や文法事項について理解しよう【知識】　英検® GTEC®

Make the correct choice to complete each sentence. （各3点）

(1) She (　　　) 18 out of 20 on the math test.
　① collected　　　② formed　　　③ picked　　　④ scored

(2) They worked together to (　　　) many popular songs.
　① achieve　　　② calculate　　　③ create　　　④ focus

(3) Spacecraft require advanced (　　　).
　① efforts　　　② prizes　　　③ technologies　　　④ victories

(4) The bottom of the pond is roughly 15 meters in (　　　).
　① deep　　　② diameter　　　③ unit　　　④ weight

(5) I won't speak to her (　　　) she apologizes to me first.
　① after　　　② since　　　③ until　　　④ while

Listening　英文を聞いて理解しよう【知識・技能】【思考力・判断力・表現力】　共通テスト　34

Listen to the English and make the best choice to match the content. （4点）

① A 15-year-old boy won the race in 2016.
② The speaker won the race in 2016.
③ It takes a lot of money to buy a drone.

Interaction　英文を聞いて会話を続けよう【知識・技能】【思考力・判断力・表現力】　スピーキング・トレーナー　35

Listen to the English and respond to the last remark. （7点）

〔メモ　　　　　　　　　　　　　　　　　　　　　　　　　　　　　　〕

🌡 **Hints**
ドローンサッカーの魅力について考えましょう。

Production (Writing)　自分の考えを書いて伝えよう【思考力・判断力・表現力】

Write your answer to the following question. （9点）

How would you like to use a drone if you got one for your birthday?

🌡 **Hints**
ドローンを使ってやってみたいことを書きましょう。

Lesson 6

A Society with Drones

Part 2
教科書 p. 94-95　　/ 50

> Drones have been used / for different purposes / for many years. // More than 70 years ago, / they were developed / for military purposes. // **Recently**, / people have found many other uses / for these unmanned aerial vehicles. //
>
> **Unfortunately**, / however, / there are some problems / with drones. // First, / some
> 5　people are against them / because they might **invade** personal privacy. // Today / more people can enjoy flying drones / than before. // Drones with high **resolution** cameras / fly taking pictures / from above. // We don't know / when secret cameras are taking shots of us, / and it may be very difficult / to protect people's privacy. //
>
> Second, / drones can have accidents / even when they are flying / in good
> 10　weather. // These aerial vehicles might **unexpectedly** fall / from the sky, / and this can hurt people / walking on the street. //
>
> (124 words)

　音読しよう　　　　　　　　　　　　　　　スピーキング・トレーナー

Practice 1　スラッシュ位置で文を区切って読んでみよう ☐
Practice 2　イントネーションに注意して読んでみよう ☐
TRY!　1分20秒以内に本文全体を音読しよう ☐

📖 Reading　本文の内容を読んで理解しよう【知識・技能】【思考力・判断力・表現力】　　(共通テスト)

Make the correct choice to complete each sentence or answer each question.　(各5点[(3)は完答])

(1) What were drones originally developed for? ☐
　① For invading others' privacy.　　② For military purposes.
　③ As unmanned transportation machines. ④ For weather research.

(2) You have learned that drones ☐.
　① can prevent accidents with high resolution cameras
　② can protect people's privacy
　③ have some negative aspects
　④ have only one use

(3) Which of the following are true? (Choose two options. The order does not matter.)
　☐ · ☐
　① Accidents don't happen as long as drones are flying in good weather.
　② Drones have never been used for military purposes.
　③ More and more people have been enjoying flying drones than before.
　④ People walking on the street might get injured by a drone crash.
　⑤ Since we know when secret cameras take pictures, we can protect our privacy easily.

🏷 Vocabulary & Grammar 　重要表現や文法事項について理解しよう【知識】　英検® GTEC®

Make the correct choice to complete each sentence. （各3点）

(1) What is the (　　　) of this experiment?
　　① idea　　　　　　② memory　　　　　③ plan　　　　　　④ purpose

(2) (　　　), this product is currently out of stock.
　　① Conveniently　　② Frequently　　　③ Traditionally　　④ Unfortunately

(3) They (　　　) the country with tanks and guns.
　　① caught　　　　　② invaded　　　　　③ moved　　　　　④ turned

(4) We enjoyed the scenery of Mt. Fuji from (　　　) on an airplane.
　　① above　　　　　② below　　　　　　③ over　　　　　　④ under

(5) (　　　) nothing to do, I went to bed earlier than usual.
　　① Had　　　　　　② Have　　　　　　③ Having　　　　　④ To have

🎧 Listening 　英文を聞いて理解しよう【知識・技能】【思考力・判断力・表現力】　共通テスト　💿 36

Listen to the English and make the best choice to match the content. （4点）
　　① Flying a drone is prohibited when strong winds are blowing.
　　② One of the causes of drone crashes is strong winds.
　　③ Traffic accidents have been increasing.

💬 Interaction 　英文を聞いて会話を続けよう【知識・技能】【思考力・判断力・表現力】　スピーキング・トレーナー　💿 37

Listen to the English and respond to the last remark. （7点）
　　〔メ モ　　　　　　　　　　　　　　　　　　　　　　　　　　　　　　　　　〕
　　🎧 **Hints**
　　ドローンの墜落事故が起きる原因を考えて話しましょう。

💬 Production (Speaking) 　自分の考えを話して伝えよう【思考力・判断力・表現力】　スピーキング・トレーナー

Answer the following question. （9点）

What do you think are the benefits of drones in our lives?
　　〔メ モ　　　　　　　　　　　　　　　　　　　　　　　　　　　　　　　　　〕
　　🎧 **Hints**
　　「Did You Know? ①ドローンとは？」（教科書 p. 92）の内容も参考にして話しましょう。

A Society with Drones

Drones have brought many benefits / to us / as well. //   In agriculture, / for example, / farmers can **sow seeds** / and spread **fertilizer** and **pesticides** / on fields / by using drones. //   This can be a great help / especially for older farmers. //   Drones may help / to solve labor shortages / and may contribute / to

5 shorter working hours, / cost **reductions**, / and improved safety. //

Also, / drones can find **survivors** / after disasters. //   Rescue workers sometimes cannot **scramble** / in **piles** of **debris** / or reach disaster areas / **contaminated** by **radiation**. //   However, / drones can fly / over such dangerous areas. //

10   Drones, / furthermore, / make our entertainment more enjoyable. //   They are used / in many concerts / and sporting events / for better camera and **lighting angles**. //   Drones might even take the place / of traditional fireworks shows / in the future. //

(122 words)

音読しよう   **スピーキング・トレーナー**

Practice 1 スラッシュ位置で文を区切って読んでみよう ☐
Practice 2 イントネーションに注意して読んでみよう ☐
TRY! 1分20秒以内に本文全体を音読しよう ☐

Reading 本文の内容を読んで理解しよう【知識・技能】【思考力・判断力・表現力】   （共通テスト）（GTEC®）

Make the correct choice to complete each sentence or answer each question. （各5点）

(1) What does "contribute" mean in line 4? ☐
　① devote　　　　② discover　　　　③ preserve　　　　④ save

(2) Drones can help farmers by ☐ .
　① flying over dangerous areas
　② growing safe and healthy crops
　③ increasing the number of young farmers
　④ sowing seeds and spreading fertilizer and pesticides on fields

(3) Which of the following is **not** true? ☐
　① Drones are used in the entertainment industry.
　② Drones can be a great help in agriculture.
　③ Drones can find survivors in disaster areas.
　④ Drones have taken the place of traditional fireworks shows.

Vocabulary & Grammar　重要表現や文法事項について理解しよう【知識】　英検® GTEC®

Make the correct choice to complete each sentence.　（各3点）

(1) She (　　　) the sunflower seeds.

　① achieved　　　② gazed　　　③ resolved　　　④ sowed

(2) There was only one (　　　) in the plane crash.

　① creator　　　② inventor　　　③ survivor　　　④ treasure

(3) Even today, rice remains the center of Japanese (　　　).

　① agriculture　　　② benefit　　　③ element　　　④ farm

(4) Chinese began to (　　　) the place of German in the language school.

　① give　　　② own　　　③ know　　　④ take

(5) John (　　　) be hungry because he has just eaten lunch.

　① cannot　　　② may　　　③ must　　　④ should

🎧 Listening　英文を聞いて理解しよう【知識・技能】【思考力・判断力・表現力】　共通テスト　💿 38

Listen to the English and make the best choice to match the content.　（4点）

① The speaker flew the drone at the Tokyo 2020 Olympics.

② The speaker saw the drone show.

③ The speaker took part in the Tokyo 2020 Olympics as an athlete.

💬 Interaction　英文を聞いて会話を続けよう【知識・技能】【思考力・判断力・表現力】　スピーキング・トレーナー　💿 39

Listen to the English and respond to the last remark.　（7点）

〔メモ　　　　　　　　　　　　　　　　　　　　　　　　　　　　　　　　　〕

🖊 **Hints**

ドローンなどの技術を農業に活用することのメリット・デメリットを考えましょう。

✍️ Production（Writing）　自分の考えを書いて伝えよう【思考力・判断力・表現力】

Write your answer to the following question.　（9点）

Do you want to see drone light shows instead of traditional fireworks shows？　Why？

🖊 **Hints**

教科書 p. 96のドローンライトショーの写真も参考にして考えましょう。

In our society / of the future, / delivery companies will use drones / to **deliver** products / more quickly and **efficiently**. // Delivery drones may help people a lot / if they have to stay home / during an **infectious** disease **pandemic**. // They may be one of the safest delivery methods / that can be used / without
5 spreading **viral** infections. //

Drones will do other jobs, / too. // **Construction** companies will use drones / to **inspect** buildings and bridges efficiently. // Since Japan's **infrastructure** is aging, / **prompt** inspections / by using drones / will be very useful. // Security companies will make use of drones / as "**bodyguards**" / in the sky. //
10 Many people may have had negative feelings / toward these flying vehicles / in the past. // However, / the future of drones / will certainly be **promising** and exciting. // Keep your eyes / on further drone **developments**! //

(128 words)

🔊)) 音読しよう 📖 〜〜〜〜〜〜〜〜〜〜〜 スピーキング・トレーナー

Practice 1 スラッシュ位置で文を区切って読んでみよう ☐
Practice 2 イントネーションに注意して読んでみよう ☐
TRY! 1分20秒以内に本文全体を音読しよう ☐

📖 Reading 本文の内容を読んで理解しよう【知識・技能】【思考力・判断力・表現力】 (共通テスト)

Make the correct choice to complete each sentence or answer each question. (各5点[(3)は完答])

(1) Which of the following industry is **not** mentioned in Part 4? ☐
　① Construction companies.　　② Delivery companies.
　③ Entertainment companies.　④ Security companies.

(2) Delivery drones will ☐.
　① be the safest delivery method when a disaster happens
　② be used as "bodyguards" in the sky
　③ deliver products more quickly and efficiently
　④ inspect buildings and bridges efficiently

(3) Which of the following are true? (Choose two options. The order does not matter.)
　☐ · ☐
　① Drones are expected to be used in a variety of industrial fields.
　② In the future, people will not have negative feelings toward drones.
　③ In the future, viral infections will spread in Japan.
　④ Japanese companies will no longer be able to use drones in their business.
　⑤ Security companies will use drones as "bodyguards."

Vocabulary & Grammar　重要表現や文法事項について理解しよう【知識】　英検®　GTEC®

Make the correct choice to complete each sentence.　(各3点)

(1) Unfortunately, your package was (　　　) to the wrong address.
　　① arrived　　　② delivered　　　③ proposed　　　④ treated

(2) That building has been under (　　　) for three years.
　　① addition　　② construction　　③ infection　　④ limitation

(3) Don't look away! (　　　) your eyes on the road when you are driving!
　　① Contact　　② Keep　　③ Look　　④ Put

(4) She is very good at singing. She is a highly (　　　) young musician.
　　① annoying　　② boring　　③ embarrassing　　④ promising

(5) I cannot find the tickets. We (　　　) them at the hotel.
　　① shouldn't have left　　　　② might have left
　　③ must not have left　　　　④ needn't have left

Listening　英文を聞いて理解しよう【知識・技能】【思考力・判断力・表現力】　共通テスト　💿 40

Listen to the English and make the best choice to match the content.　(4点)
　　① The drone market size in 2024 is expected to be about as large as it was in 2020.
　　② The drone market size in 2024 is expected to be less than 220 billion yen.
　　③ The drone market size in 2024 is expected to be over 500 billion yen.

Interaction　英文を聞いて会話を続けよう【知識・技能】【思考力・判断力・表現力】　スピーキング・トレーナー　💿 41

Listen to the English and respond to the remarks.　(7点)
〔メ モ　　　　　　　　　　　　　　　　　　　　　　　　　　　　　　〕

🔔 **Hints**
That's because ... (なぜなら…だからだ)

Production (Writing)　自分の考えを書いて伝えよう【思考力・判断力・表現力】

Write your answer to the following question.　(9点)
How do you think drones will change our lives in the future?

_____

_____

🔔 **Hints**
ドローンの未来や可能性について書きましょう。

"Super **Clone** Cultural **Properties**" Special Exhibition //

You will find a lot of important **insights** / when you encounter our "cloned" **artworks**: / "Super Clone Cultural Properties." //

Dates: November 18 / to December 28 //

5 Opening hours: 10:00－17:30 //

(Admission ends / 30 minutes before closing time.) //

Closed: Mondays / (**except** national holidays) //

Place: The **Basement Gallery** / of Daiichi Bldg. //

Admission: Adult (**general**) ¥800 //

10 Student* ¥400 //

Child (age 12 and under) Free //

Senior (age 65 and older)* ¥400 //

*A **discount** is **available** / if you show a photo ID. //

For further information, / visit the following site: / www.daiichigallery.org //

15 *David:* What are you looking at, / Kumi? //

Kumi: This is about a special art exhibition. //

David: Sounds interesting! //

Kumi: Do you know anything / about "cloned" artworks? //

David: Hmm … / I don't think / I do. //

20 *Kumi:* Then, / why don't we go to the gallery together / this weekend? //

(127 words)

🔊 音読しよう

スピーキング・トレーナー

Practice 1 スラッシュ位置で文を区切って読んでみよう ☐
Practice 2 英語の音の変化に注意して読んでみよう ☐
TRY! 1分20秒以内に本文全体を音読しよう ☐

📖 **Reading** 本文の内容を読んで理解しよう【知識・技能】【思考力・判断力・表現力】 共通テスト

Make the correct choice to complete each sentence or answer each question. ((1)は7点, (2)は8点)

(1) What is the last admission time for this exhibition? ☐

① At 9:30 a.m. ② At 10:00 a.m. ③ At 5:00 p.m. ④ At 5:30 p.m.

(2) If you want to get a student discount, you should ☐.

① bring your photo ID ② buy the ticket on the website

③ enter the gallery after 5 p.m. ④ visit the gallery on a national holiday

🔊 英語の音の変化を理解して音読することができる。　📖 展覧会に関する広告と対話文を読んで概要や要点をとらえることができる。
📰 文脈を理解して適切な語句を用いて英文を完成することができる。　🎧 平易な英語で話される短い英文を聞いて必要な情報を聞き取ることができる。
💬 芸術作品について簡単な語句を用いて情報や考えを伝えることができる。　✍️ 芸術作品について簡単な語句を用いて考えを表現することができる。

Vocabulary & Grammar 重要表現や文法事項について理解しよう【知識】　英検® GTEC®

Make the correct choice to complete each sentence. （各3点）

(1) The explorer (　　　) many adventures on the way.
　① bought　　　　② encountered　　　③ experimented　　　④ visited

(2) If you sign up as a member, you can get a 10 percent (　　　) anytime.
　① discount　　　② fare　　　③ fee　　　④ money

(3) The restaurant is open every day (　　　) Sunday.
　① during　　　② except　　　③ unless　　　④ without

(4) Are there any tickets (　　　) for tonight's musical?
　① available　　　② capable　　　③ enable　　　④ sustainable

(5) (　　　) you were not at the meeting, we made the decision without you.
　① Until　　　② If　　　③ Since　　　④ Unless

Listening 英文を聞いて理解しよう【知識・技能】【思考力・判断力・表現力】　共通テスト　💿 42

Listen to the English and make the best choice to match the content. （4点）

① The British Museum is the most popular museum in the world.
② The speaker has been to the British Museum.
③ The speaker wants to go to the British Museum.

Interaction 英文を聞いて会話を続けよう【知識・技能】【思考力・判断力・表現力】　スピーキング・トレーナー　💿 43

Listen to the English and respond to the last remark. （7点）

〔メ モ　　　　　　　　　　　　　　　　　　　　　　　　　　　　　　　　　〕

👆**Hints**
I would like to [want to] see ... で始めて，見てみたい芸術作品を答えましょう。

Production（Writing） 自分の考えを書いて伝えよう【思考力・判断力・表現力】

Write your answer to the following question. （9点）

What art work were you impressed by most and in what way?

👆**Hints**
感銘を受けた芸術作品について書きましょう。

It is very hard / to keep cultural properties / as they are. // Some are damaged / during **conflicts**. // Attacked by the Taliban, / statues and **ceiling** paintings / of Buddhas / at Bamiyan / in Afghanistan / were **destroyed** / in 2001. // Others are **harmed** / due to **tourists**. // Buddhist **caves** / in Dunhuang, /
5 China, / are gradually being damaged / by the large numbers of tourists. //

How can we **preserve** cultural properties / and show them / to the public? // "Super Clone Cultural Properties" / can solve this problem. // **Professor** Masaaki Miyasako is a **pioneer** / in this "cloning" technology. // He tries to revive artworks / of all ages and countries. //

10 Some people have negative opinions / about "copied" art. // However, / Miyasako's team respects the DNA / of the original artworks. // The production process / of cloning artworks / is quite different / from copying things. //

(125 words)

🔊) 音読しよう 📖

Practice 1 スラッシュ位置で文を区切って読んでみよう ☐
Practice 2 英語の音の変化に注意して読んでみよう ☐
TRY! 1分20秒以内に本文全体を音読しよう ☐

スピーキング・トレーナー

📖 Reading 本文の内容を読んで理解しよう【知識・技能】【思考力・判断力・表現力】 共通テスト GTEC®

Make the correct choice to complete each sentence or answer each question. (各5点)

(1) Buddhist caves in Dunhuang, China, ☐.
　① are being damaged by tourists
　② are being damaged by a lot of storms
　③ were destroyed by a fire
　④ were destroyed by the Taliban

(2) What does "pioneer" mean in line 8? ☐
　① collector　　　② messenger　　　③ originator　　　④ voyager

(3) Which of the following is **not** true? ☐
　① Cultural properties are damaged for a variety of reasons.
　② Miyasako is a pioneer in "cloning" technology to revive Japanese artworks.
　③ Producing cloning artworks differs from copying.
　④ Some people have negative feelings toward "copying" art.

Vocabulary & Grammar 重要表現や文法事項について理解しよう【知識】 英検® GTEC®

Make the correct choice to complete each sentence. (各3点)

(1) You can expect a (　　　) of opinion between those two men.

① conflict　　　　② director　　　　③ pressure　　　　④ relationship

(2) The whole town was (　　　) by the big earthquake.

① broken　　　　② destroyed　　　　③ examined　　　　④ stayed

(3) You can (　　　) fruit by making it into jam.

① collect　　　　② maintain　　　　③ offer　　　　④ preserve

(4) Ken arrived late (　　　) the storm.

① according to　　② due to　　　　③ in charge of　　④ in order to

(5) (　　　) by my older brother, I started to ride a skateboard.

① Influence　　　② Influenced　　　③ Influencing　　　④ To influence

Listening 英文を聞いて理解しよう【知識・技能】【思考力・判断力・表現力】 共通テスト 🔘 44

Listen to the English and make the best choice to match the content. (4点)

① Artworks need to be restored regularly.

② Experts are trying to preserve artworks.

③ Some artworks are really valuable.

Interaction 英文を聞いて会話を続けよう【知識・技能】【思考力・判断力・表現力】 スピーキング・トレーナー 🔘 45

Listen to the English and respond to the last remark. (7点)

〔メ モ　　　　　　　　　　　　　　　　　　　　　　　　　　　　　　　　　　　　　〕

🌡 **Hints**

Japanese wolf (ニホンオオカミ), Lutra nippon (ニホンカワウソ), mammoth (マンモス)

Production (Writing) 自分の考えを書いて伝えよう【思考力・判断力・表現力】

Write your answer to the following question. (9点)

What do you think about reviving extinct species with cloning technology?

🌡 **Hints**

academic research (学術研究), dinosaur (恐竜), revive (…を生き返らせる)

Lesson 7

"Cloning" Cultural Properties

In 2017, / Miyasako's team succeeded / in cloning the *Shaka Triad* statue / of Horyuji Temple. // Team members not only **reproduced** the statue / but also **restored** missing parts. //

There were difficulties / which Miyasako had to get over. // His team was not
5 able to take pictures / of the back of the statue. // In order to clone the statue, / team members **complemented** information / about it / by using saved data / and **academic** insights. // Miyasako said, / "We aim to revive the statue, / **referring** to professionals' advice / and old books." //

When the statue was first created, / it was probably **shining** gold. // Miyasako
10 wants to clone the statue / even more **closely** to the original / the next time. // He thinks / that his cloned artwork should **convey** the hearts / of the **creators** / at that time. //

(125 words)

Practice 1 スラッシュ位置で文を区切って読んでみよう ☐
Practice 2 英語の音の変化に注意して読んでみよう ☐
TRY! 1分20秒以内に本文全体を音読しよう ☐

📖 Reading 本文の内容を読んで理解しよう【知識・技能】【思考力・判断力・表現力】 (共通テスト)

Make the correct choice to complete each sentence or answer each question. (各5点)

(1) In 2017, what did Miyasako and his team succeed in? ☐
  ① In cloning the Buddhist cave at Horyuji Temple.
  ② In cloning the ceiling painting of Buddhas.
  ③ In cloning the *Shaka Triad* statue of Horyuji Temple.
  ④ In cloning the *Shaka Triad* statue of Todaiji Temple.

(2) Which of the following is one of the difficulties that Miyasako's team had to get over? ☐
  ① They couldn't have access to academic insights from the *Shaka Triad* statue.
  ② They couldn't paint the *Shaka Triad* statue gold.
  ③ They couldn't revive the *Shaka Triad* statue.
  ④ They couldn't take pictures of the back of the *Shaka Triad* statue.

(3) Miyasako thinks that cloned artwork should ☐.
  ① be as valuable as the original ones
  ② be shining gold at all times
  ③ convey the hearts of the creators at that time
  ④ look more gorgeous than the original ones

🎴 Vocabulary & Grammar　重要表現や文法事項について理解しよう【知識】　英検®　GTEC®

Make the correct choice to complete each sentence.　（各3点）

(1) John (　　　) in getting into the university.
　① scrambled　　　② spent　　　③ succeeded　　　④ tried

(2) She often refers (　　　) the English dictionary in order to check spelling.
　① in　　　② on　　　③ to　　　④ with

(3) A truck (　　　) my furniture to my new house.
　① attached　　　② conveyed　　　③ introduced　　　④ reached

(4) The castle has been (　　　) and is open to the public.
　① decreased　　　② reported　　　③ restored　　　④ translated

(5) This is the hospital (　　　) my mother works at.
　① how　　　② what　　　③ where　　　④ which

🎧 Listening　英文を聞いて理解しよう【知識・技能】【思考力・判断力・表現力】　共通テスト　💿46

Listen to the English and make the best choice to match the content.　（4点）

　① A painting was unsuccessfully restored.
　② The speaker is an artist.
　③ The speaker lives in Spain.

💬 Interaction　英文を聞いて会話を続けよう【知識・技能】【思考力・判断力・表現力】　スピーキング・トレーナー　💿47

Listen to the English and respond to the remark.　（7点）

〔メ モ　　　　　　　　　　　　　　　　　　　　　　　　　　　　　　　〕

🕐 **Hints**
landscape (風景画)，oil painting (油絵)，portrait (肖像画)，sculpture (彫刻)

😀 Production (Speaking)　自分の考えを話して伝えよう【思考力・判断力・表現力】　スピーキング・トレーナー

Answer the following question.　（9点）

Who is your favorite painter?

〔メ モ　　　　　　　　　　　　　　　　　　　　　　　　　　　　　　　〕

🕐 **Hints**
Taro Okamoto (岡本太郎)，Pablo Picasso (パブロ・ピカソ)，Vincent van Gogh (フィンセント・ファン・ゴッホ)

Lesson 7

"Cloning" Cultural Properties

Miyasako also reproduced / Tawaraya Sotatsu's *Cherry Blossoms and Poppies*. // His team used a camera / with which all the **details** of the painting / could be collected. // Thanks to the cloning technology, / people can see the cloned work / in its original place / at all times. // At the same time, / the
5 original can be preserved / in a different place. //

The **Fifer**, / a famous painting / by Edouard Manet, / was reproduced / not only as a painting / but also as a statue. // At an exhibition, / even those who could not see well / could touch the statue / and appreciate the work. //

When Miyasako clones cultural properties, / he values traditional **techniques** / of **artisanship**. // He also uses the latest technologies. // With the cloning
10 technology, / we may be able to preserve cultural properties / and make them available / to the public / forever. //

(131 words)

 音読しよう　　　　　　　　　　　　　　スピーキング・トレーナー

Practice 1 スラッシュ位置で文を区切って読んでみよう ☐
Practice 2 英語の音の変化に注意して読んでみよう ☐
TRY! 1分20秒以内に本文全体を音読しよう ☐

Reading　本文の内容を読んで理解しよう【知識・技能】【思考力・判断力・表現力】　　共通テスト

Make the correct choice to complete each sentence or answer each question.　((1)は7点, (2)は8点)

(1) *The Fifer*, a famous painting by Edouard Manet, was reproduced ☐.

① as a painting for people who cannot see well

② because the work was really valuable

③ both as a painting and a statue

④ not only as a photograph but also as a statue

(2) Which of the following is **not** true? ☐

① Cloning technology allows people to see the cloned work in its original place at all times while the original one is preserved in a different place.

② Miyasako never uses traditional techniques of artisanship in cloning cultural properties.

③ Miyasako used a camera to reproduce *Cherry Blossoms and Poppies*.

④ Thanks to cloning technology, we may be able to see cultural properties forever.

Goals

🔊 英語の音の変化を理解して音読することができる。　📖 クローン作品に関する英文を読んで概要や要点をとらえることができる。
📑 文脈を理解して適切な語句を用いて英文を完成することができる。　🎧 平易な英語で話される短い英文を聞いて必要な情報を聞き取ることができる。
💬 クローン作品について簡単な語句を用いて情報や考えを伝えることができる。　✍ 芸術について簡単な語句を用いて考えを表現することができる。

Vocabulary & Grammar　重要表現や文法事項について理解しよう【知識】　　英検® GTEC®

Make the correct choice to complete each sentence.　（各3点）

(1) Our English teacher taught us English grammar in (　　　).

　① detail　　　② expert　　　③ response　　　④ section

(2) The train station has been restored to its (　　　) condition.

　① clever　　　② enormous　　　③ original　　　④ polite

(3) This book is for (　　　) who are interested in fishing.

　① one　　　② that　　　③ these　　　④ those

(4) His book is highly (　　　) by historians.

　① cured　　　② invented　　　③ suffered　　　④ valued

(5) The professor told the student, "Read the passage (　　　) I referred in my lecture."

　① that　　　② to that　　　③ to which　　　④ which

🎧 Listening　英文を聞いて理解しよう【知識・技能】【思考力・判断力・表現力】　　共通テスト　💿48

Listen to the English and make the best choice to match the content.　（4点）

　① The speaker is going to organize the exhibition.

　② The speaker is going to show her work in the exhibition.

　③ The speaker is going to visit the Nagano Prefectural Museum of Art.

💬 Interaction　英文を聞いて会話を続けよう【知識・技能】【思考力・判断力・表現力】　スピーキング・トレーナー　💿49

Listen to the English and respond to the remark.　（7点）

〔メ モ 　　　　　　　　　　　　　　　　　　　　　　　　　　　　　　　　〕

🔑**Hints**
スーパークローン文化財の将来像を自由に想像してみましょう。

✍ Production（Writing）　自分の考えを書いて伝えよう【思考力・判断力・表現力】

Write your answer to the following question.　（9点）

Write about the artistic things you want to experience by the time you turn 30.

🔑**Hints**
30歳になるまでに鑑賞しておきたい芸術や音楽について書きましょう。

"The use of **atomic** energy / for purposes of war / is a crime. // It is **immoral**." // **Pope** Francis said this / at Hiroshima Peace Memorial Park / on November 24, 2019. // On that day, / the Meeting for Peace was held / in front of the **Cenotaph** for the **A-bomb** Victims. //

5 About 2,000 people attended the meeting. // Among them was a Japanese High School Student Peace Ambassador. // She handed the Pope a light, / and he lit a **candle**. // She had met him before / in the Vatican / and had asked him / to come to Hiroshima. // She said, / "I'm happy / if our wish made his visit possible." //

10 At the meeting, / the Pope gave his message / to the world. // "Never again war, / never again the **clash** of arms, / never again so much **suffering**! // May peace come / in our time / and to our world." //

(135 words)

音読しよう　**スピーキング・トレーナー**

Practice 1 スラッシュ位置で文を区切って読んでみよう ☐
Practice 2 英語の音の変化に注意して読んでみよう ☐
TRY! 1分20秒以内に本文全体を音読しよう ☐

Reading　本文の内容を読んで理解しよう【知識・技能】【思考力・判断力・表現力】　共通テスト

Make the correct choice to complete each sentence or answer each question. ((1)は 7 点, (2)は完答 8 点)

(1) A Japanese high school student ☐.

① attended the Meeting for Peace
② gave her speech in front of the Pope
③ lit a candle during the Meeting for Peace
④ met the Pope at the Meeting for Peace for the first time

(2) Which of the following are true? (Choose two options. The order does not matter.)
☐ · ☐

① At the Meeting for Peace, the Pope emphasized the importance of nuclear energy.
② The Meeting for Peace was held on November 24, 2019.
③ The Pope insisted that atomic energy should be used effectively, except for war.
④ The Pope invited a Japanese High School Student Peace Ambassador to the Vatican.
⑤ The Pope expressed the need for peace in the world.

📇 Vocabulary & Grammar　重要表現や文法事項について理解しよう【知識】　(英検®) (GTEC®)

Make the correct choice to complete each sentence.　(各3点)

(1) Even if you don't get caught, stealing is still (　　　　).
　① artificial　　　② classical　　　③ facial　　　④ immoral

(2) Sorry, I can't (　　　) tomorrow's meeting.
　① attach　　　② attempt　　　③ attend　　　④ attract

(3) There was a serious (　　　) of opinions at the meeting last night.
　① accident　　　② clash　　　③ match　　　④ war

(4) Brian studied (　　　) reactions in his physics course.
　① atomic　　　② energetic　　　③ fuel　　　④ power

(5) At the foot of her bed (　　　) with a baby in it.
　① a cradle was　　② a cradle where　　③ was a cradle　　④ where a cradle

🎧 Listening　英文を聞いて理解しよう【知識・技能】【思考力・判断力・表現力】　(共通テスト) 💿 50

Listen to the English and make the best choice to match the content.　(4点)
　① The speaker is going to make a speech in English.
　② The speaker wants to become a Japanese High School Student Peace Ambassador.
　③ The speaker went to the United Nations Office.

💬 Interaction　英文を聞いて会話を続けよう【知識・技能】【思考力・判断力・表現力】　スピーキング・トレーナー 💿 51

Listen to the English and respond to the last remark.　(7点)
　〔メモ　　　　　　　　　　　　　　　　　　　　　　　　　　　　　　　　　〕

👆**Hints**
講演会だけではなく，動画サイトなどで聞いたことがあるものも含めて考えましょう。

✍ Production (Writing)　自分の考えを書いて伝えよう【思考力・判断力・表現力】

Write your answer to the following question.　(9点)

What do you think the Japanese High School Student Peace Ambassador felt when she met the Pope in the Vatican?

👆**Hints**
高校生平和大使の立場になって考えましょう。be proud of ... (…を誇りに思う), honorable (名誉ある), nervous (緊張している)

Lesson 8

Peace Messages from Hiroshima

Setsuko Thurlow also took part / in the Meeting for Peace. // When she was 13, / she experienced the atomic **bombing** / in Hiroshima. // Her sister and **nephew,** / as well as many of her classmates, / lost their lives / at that time. //

Thurlow believed / that her experience / as an A-bomb survivor / would play
5　an important role. // She started a nuclear **disarmament campaign** / in the 1950s. // She gave a lot of **lectures** / **throughout** the world. // Her activities even influenced world leaders. //

Thurlow listened to Pope Francis speak / at the meeting. // She hoped / that his appeal for world peace / would help people **seek** it / even more. // She said, /
10　"I'm sure / his message will spread / all over the world. // Every citizen must take his message / as a starting point / and take action / to **eliminate** nuclear weapons." //

(129 words)

音読しよう

スピーキング・トレーナー

Practice 1 スラッシュ位置で文を区切って読んでみよう ☐
Practice 2 英語の音の変化に注意して読んでみよう ☐
TRY! 1分15秒以内に本文全体を音読しよう ☐

Reading 本文の内容を読んで理解しよう【知識・技能】【思考力・判断力・表現力】 (共通テスト)

Make the correct choice to complete each sentence or answer each question. (各5点[(1)は完答])

(1) Put the following events (①〜④) into the order in which they happened.

☐ → ☐ → ☐ → ☐

① Thurlow experienced the atomic bombing.
② Thurlow lost her relatives and classmates.
③ Thurlow participated in the Meeting for Peace.
④ Thurlow started a nuclear disarmament campaign.

(2) Thurlow wanted ☐.

① people to continue to tell about her A-bomb experience
② people to join her nuclear disarmament campaign
③ people to seek world peace
④ the Pope to give a lot of lectures to eliminate nuclear weapons

(3) Which of the following is **not** true? ☐

① Some world leaders were influenced by Thurlow's activities.
② Thurlow is against nuclear weapons.
③ Thurlow listened to the Pope's speech at the Meeting for Peace.
④ Thurlow's parents died in the atomic bombing in Hiroshima.

Vocabulary & Grammar 　重要表現や文法事項について理解しよう【知識】　　英検® 　GTEC®

Make the correct choice to complete each sentence. （各3点）

(1) Mandela (　　　) a leading role in ending apartheid.
　① felt 　　　　② made 　　　　③ passed 　　　　④ played

(2) He and his team went on a voyage to (　　　) unknown lands.
　① arrive 　　　② determine 　　　③ seek 　　　　④ unite

(3) That (　　　) was so boring that I almost fell asleep.
　① costume 　　② language 　　③ lecture 　　　④ restaurant

(4) Japan took part (　　　) the Olympics for the first time in 1912.
　① in 　　　　　② of 　　　　　③ to 　　　　　④ with

(5) Shall I have him (　　　) you back later?
　① call 　　　　② called 　　　③ calling 　　　④ to call

Listening 　英文を聞いて理解しよう【知識・技能】【思考力・判断力・表現力】　　共通テスト 　52

Listen to the English and make the best choice to match the content. （4点）

① ICAN is an international organization that creates nuclear weapons.
② ICAN received the Nobel Peace Prize in 2017.
③ The speaker was awarded the Nobel Peace Prize in 2017.

Interaction 　英文を聞いて会話を続けよう【知識・技能】【思考力・判断力・表現力】　　スピーキング・トレーナー 　53

Listen to the English and respond to the last remark. （7点）

〔メモ　　　　　　　　　　　　　　　　　　　　　　　　　　　　　　　　　　　　　〕

Hints
collect signature (署名を集める), realize (…を実現する), weapon (武器)

Production (Writing) 　自分の考えを書いて伝えよう【思考力・判断力・表現力】

Write your answer to the following question. （9点）

Why do you think nuclear weapons cannot be eliminated from the world?

Hints
advantage (利点), attack (…を攻撃する), diplomacy (外交)

Lesson 8

Peace Messages from Hiroshima

In 2016, / Barack Obama, / the U.S. president / and the 2009 Nobel **Laureate** in Peace, / came to Hiroshima. // He was the first **sitting** president / to visit the atomic-bombed city. // He knew / atomic bomb survivors were getting older / and said / in his speech, "Someday / the voices of the *hibakusha* / will no longer

5 be with us / to bear **witness**." //

Obama **emphasized** the importance of science. // He **insisted** / that science should be focused / on improving life, / not eliminating it. // This is part of the lesson of Hiroshima. // We shouldn't keep our eyes turned away / from the lesson / anymore. //

In his speech, / Obama called on world leaders / to choose a world / with no

10 more war. // "Hiroshima and Nagasaki are known / not as the **dawn** / of atomic **warfare**, / but as the start / of our own **moral awakening**." // This is the future, / Obama said, / "we can choose." //

(140 words)

音読しよう   **スピーキング・トレーナー**

Practice 1 スラッシュ位置で文を区切って読んでみよう ☐
Practice 2 英語の音の変化に注意して読んでみよう ☐
TRY! 1分20秒以内に本文全体を音読しよう ☐

Reading 本文の内容を読んで理解しよう【知識・技能】【思考力・判断力・表現力】   共通テスト GTEC®

Make the correct choice to complete each sentence or answer each question. （各5点[(3)は完答]）

(1) What does "witness" mean in line 5? ☐
　① evidence　　② practice　　③ statistics　　④ theory

(2) Obama said that Hiroshima and Nagasaki are known ☐.
　① as the start of our own moral awakening, not as the dawn of atomic warfare
　② either as the dawn of a nuclear war or as the start of our own moral awakening
　③ neither as the dawn of a nuclear war nor as the start of our own moral awakening
　④ not only as the dawn of atomic warfare, but also as the start of our own moral awakening

(3) Which of the following are true? (Choose two options. The order does not matter.)
　☐ · ☐
　① Obama came to Hiroshima in 2009 and won the Nobel Peace Prize in 2016.
　② Obama claimed that we shouldn't look away from the lesson of Hiroshima anymore.
　③ Obama didn't know the *hibakusha* were getting older.
　④ Obama insisted that science should be used to improve our lives.
　⑤ Obama visited Hiroshima as a former U.S. president.

🔊 英語の音の変化を理解して音読することができる。　📖 オバマ元大統領のメッセージに関する英文を読んで概要や要点をとらえることができる。
📑 文脈を理解して適切な語句を用いて英文を完成することができる。　🎧 平易な英語で話される短い英文を聞いて必要な情報を聞き取ることができる。
📝 被爆体験について簡単な語句を用いて情報や考えを伝えることができる。　🖊 戦争体験について簡単な語句を用いて考えを表現することができる。

🏷 Vocabulary & Grammar　重要表現や文法事項について理解しよう【知識】　英検® GTEC®

Make the correct choice to complete each sentence. （各3点）

(1) We were good friends once, but we are (　　　) longer friends now.
① any ② anymore ③ no ④ not

(2) It was very cold, but he (　　　) on keeping the door open.
① called ② insisted ③ provided ④ wished

(3) We can't completely (　　　) fat from our daily meals.
① discriminate ② eliminate ③ erase ④ reverse

(4) The world leaders (　　　) both sides to agree to end the war.
① brought up ② called on ③ took off ④ put off

(5) A lot of people saw him (　　　) on the street.
① arrests ② arrested ③ was arresting ④ to be arrested

🎧 Listening　英文を聞いて理解しよう【知識・技能】【思考力・判断力・表現力】　共通テスト 🔘54

Listen to the English and make the best choice to match the content. （4点）

① The speaker listened to Obama's speech at Hiroshima Peace Memorial Park.
② The speaker read an article about Obama's speech.
③ The speaker wrote a newspaper article about Obama's speech.

💬 Interaction　英文を聞いて会話を続けよう【知識・技能】【思考力・判断力・表現力】　スピーキング・トレーナー 🔘55

Listen to the English and respond to the last remark. （7点）

〔メモ　　　　　　　　　　　　　　　　　　　　　　　　　　　　　　　　　　　　〕

🌡**Hints**
Yes の場合はそのとき感じたことなどを，No の場合は被爆者からどんな話を聞いてみたいかを答えましょう。

🖊 Production（Writing）　自分の考えを書いて伝えよう【思考力・判断力・表現力】

Write your answer to the following question. （9点）

Do you think it is necessary to share the experience of war with younger generations?
Why?

🌡**Hints**
in the past（過去に），tragic（悲惨な）

Lesson 8
Peace Messages from Hiroshima

David: The media reported a lot / on the Pope's message / in Hiroshima. //　The question is, / will the message help / to get **rid** of nuclear weapons? //

Kumi: Not **immediately**. //　But the Pope's visit is a **significant** step. //

Manabu: Yes, / his call to **abolish** nuclear weapons / spread all over the world. //

5　*Vivian:* He said, / "How can we speak of peace / even as we build **terrifying** new weapons?" //　Very **impressive**. //

David: Do you think / world leaders will listen / and share the ideal of peace / with him? //

Kumi: I'm not sure. //　But we should realize the fact / that younger people / like

10　us / will be leaders someday. //　The world will gradually change. //

David: How true! //　So, / what can you do now? //

Vivian: We have to learn more / about peace and war. //　We should also learn / to have high morals / to **deal** with **scientific** developments. //

(131 words)

音読しよう

スピーキング・トレーナー

Practice 1　スラッシュ位置で文を区切って読んでみよう ☐
Practice 2　英語の音の変化に注意して読んでみよう ☐
TRY!　1分15秒以内に本文全体を音読しよう ☐

📖 Reading　本文の内容を読んで理解しよう【知識・技能】【思考力・判断力・表現力】

共通テスト　GTEC®

Make the correct choice to complete each sentence or answer each question.　(各5点)

(1)　What does "call" mean in line 4?　☐
　　① demand　　　　② dream　　　　③ phone　　　　④ visit

(2)　In order to abolish nuclear weapons, Vivian thinks we should ☐.
　　① build terrifying new weapons
　　② learn to have high morals to deal with scientific developments as well as learn more about peace and war
　　③ realize the fact that younger people will be leaders
　　④ share the ideal of peace with the Pope

(3)　Which of the following is **not** true?　☐
　　① Kumi thinks the world will gradually change.
　　② Students are discussing the Pope's message.
　　③ The Pope's visit is a significant step.
　　④ World leaders immediately shared their ideals of peace with the Pope.

Vocabulary & Grammar　重要表現や文法事項について理解しよう【知識】　英検® GTEC®

Make the correct choice to complete each sentence.　（各3点）

(1) There were lots of fantastic displays, but the most (　　　　) was the Japanese garden.
① active　　　　② expensive　　　　③ impressive　　　　④ positive

(2) The economist said the Japanese government should (　　　　) the sales tax.
① abolish　　　　② congratulate　　　　③ recover　　　　④ share

(3) He opened the door to (　　　　) of the smell of tobacco.
① get rid　　　　② lose sight　　　　③ make fun　　　　④ run out

(4) How do you (　　　　) this problem?
① deal with　　　　② hold on　　　　③ manage to　　　　④ throw away

(5) Mr. Brown received the news (　　　　) his daughter was accepted to the university.
① on　　　　② of　　　　③ that　　　　④ what

🎧 Listening　英文を聞いて理解しよう【知識・技能】【思考力・判断力・表現力】　共通テスト　💿 56

Listen to the English and make the best choice to match the content.　（4点）
① Both Japanese people and non-Japanese people attend the Peace Memorial Ceremony.
② The speaker goes abroad every year on August 6.
③ The speaker has never attended the Peace Memorial Ceremony.

💬 Interaction　英文を聞いて会話を続けよう【知識・技能】【思考力・判断力・表現力】　スピーキング・トレーナー　💿 57

Listen to the English and respond to the remarks.　（7点）

〔メモ　　　　　　　　　　　　　　　　　　　　　　　　　　　　　　　　　　　　　〕

🎐 **Hints**
「いつ学んだか」と「どのように感じたか」の2点が聞かれていることを押さえましょう。

✍️ Production (Writing)　自分の考えを書いて伝えよう【思考力・判断力・表現力】

Write your answer to the following question.　（9点）

If you could meet someone who has contributed to peace and human rights, who would you like to meet and what would you like to talk about with him or her?

🎐 **Hints**
Abraham Lincoln（エイブラハム・リンカーン）, Malala Yousafzai（マララ・ユスフザイ）, Nelson Mandela（ネルソン・マンデラ）

A cooking competition / among high school students / in Hokkaido / **invigorates** the local community. // The competition is called "The **Challenge Gourmet** Contest." // In this contest, / high school students compete / in making their own original recipes / and using their cooking skills / while using local

5 **ingredients**. //

Students **flexibly** develop their ideas / to create recipes / for the contest. // On the day of the contest, / **contestants** serve their original food / to local people. // A **panel** of judges tries all the food, / **selects** their favorites, / and records their votes. // **Consequently**, / this type of contest brings energy / to the local

10 community / through food. //

A man / in a local **fishermen**'s organization / says, / "The contest is one of the biggest events / in this town." // The high school students / entertain the **townspeople**. // At the same time, / the students learn a lot more / from participating in a community event. //

(138 words)

🔊)) 音読しよう 📖 ～～～～～～～～～～ スピーキング・トレーナー

Practice 1 スラッシュ位置で文を区切って読んでみよう □
Practice 2 音声を聞きながら，音声のすぐ後を追って読んでみよう □
TRY! 1分20秒以内に本文全体を音読しよう □

📖 **Reading** 本文の内容を読んで理解しよう【知識・技能】【思考力・判断力・表現力】 (共通テスト)(GTEC®)

Make the correct choice to complete each sentence or answer each question. （各5点）

(1) What does "entertain" mean in line 12? ☐
　① amuse　　　　② bore　　　　③ excite　　　　④ relax

(2) In the Challenge Gourmet Contest, ☐ .
　① high school students make their original recipes with local ingredients
　② local people compete using their cooking skills
　③ local people serve their original food to high school students
　④ only high school students who have high cooking skills make their original recipes

(3) Which of the following is **not** true? ☐
　① Judges of the contest taste all the dishes, choose their favorites and record their votes.
　② The high school students learn a lot from the community event.
　③ On the day of the contest, participants provide local residents with foods they cook.
　④ This kind of contest brings jobs to the community.

Vocabulary & Grammar 　重要表現や文法事項について理解しよう【知識】　英検® GTEC®

Make the correct choice to complete each sentence. （各3点）

(1) The two young boys (　　　) with each other for Julia's love.
　① compete　　② create　　③ replace　　④ surround

(2) Yoga exercises can help either relax or (　　) your body.
　① decrease　　② invigorate　　③ remove　　④ rise

(3) Ellen (　　) the book from the top shelf.
　① continued　　② prevented　　③ recorded　　④ selected

(4) Japan is facing various (　　) due to its declining birthrate.
　① businesses　　② challenges　　③ diseases　　④ systems

(5) Though (　　), he worked till late at night.
　① tire　　② tired　　③ tiring　　④ to be tired

Listening 　英文を聞いて理解しよう【知識・技能】【思考力・判断力・表現力】　共通テスト 🔵58

Listen to the English and make the best choice to match the content. （4点）
　① All the local governments in Japan have their own mascots.
　② Local mascots are loved only by children.
　③ Local mascots help their community become invigorated.

Interaction 　英文を聞いて会話を続けよう【知識・技能】【思考力・判断力・表現力】　スピーキング・トレーナー 🔵59

Listen to the English and respond to the remark. （7点）
〔メモ　　　　　　　　　　　　　　　　　　　　　〕

🔔Hints
Yes の場合は，参加した大会やコンテストについて具体的に話しましょう。No の場合は，参加してみたい大会やコンテストについて話しましょう。

Production (Speaking) 　自分の考えを話して伝えよう【思考力・判断力・表現力】　スピーキング・トレーナー

Answer the following question. （9点）
Choose some events in your town and describe which one you like the best.
〔メモ　　　　　　　　　　　　　　　　　　　　　〕

🔔Hints
Local Foods Festival (地元食材祭り)，Morning Market (朝市)，Sports Day (運動会)

High school students / in the contest / get **valuable** training / to enter the adult world. // In managing to **organize** an event / with local adults, / they can get an **opportunity** / to change / from "being served and cared for" / to "serving and caring for" someone. // As a result, / they realize / that society needs them. //

5   Local people hope / that high school students will make **contributions** / to their communities. // Today's **aging** society often leads to **declines** / in local industries. // Many people think / that the power of **youths** is **indispensable** / for solving local problems / and for **maintaining** the special values / of their communities. //

10   Young people have their own **outstanding** ideas / and the **vitality** / to create new things. // They can show their new ways of thinking / without sticking to old customs. // In the "gourmet contest," / such **characteristics** / of the high school students / seem to have created interesting and delicious food. //

(143 words)

🔊)) 音読しよう 📖 ～～～～～～～～～～～～～ スピーキング・トレーナー

Practice 1 スラッシュ位置で文を区切って読んでみよう ☐
Practice 2 音声を聞きながら，音声のすぐ後を追って読んでみよう ☐
TRY! 1分20秒以内に本文全体を音読しよう ☐

📖 **Reading** 本文の内容を読んで理解しよう【知識・技能】【思考力・判断力・表現力】 共通テスト GTEC®

Make the correct choice to complete each sentence or answer each question. (各5点)

(1) What does "indispensable" mean in line 7? ☐
  ① additional   ② essential   ③ needless   ④ superior

(2) When high school students manage to organize an event in their local community, ☐ .
  ① they contribute to declines in local industries
  ② they feel that they are needed by society
  ③ they have a chance to change from caring for someone to being cared for
  ④ they realize that they need local adults

(3) Which of the following is true? ☐
  ① Local people hope that high school students will contribute to their communities.
  ② Students can show their new ways of thinking by sticking to old customs.
  ③ The power of youths is necessary for solving food waste problems.
  ④ Today's aging society often brings growth in local industries.

Vocabulary & Grammar 重要表現や文法事項について理解しよう【知識】 (英検®) (GTEC®)

Make the correct choice to complete each sentence. （各3点）

(1) Do you have much (　　　) to speak English?

　① character 　② moment 　③ opportunity 　④ schedule

(2) My older sister cared (　　　) me when I was sick in bed.

　① after 　② by 　③ for 　④ of

(3) The writer made a great (　　　) to creating an English dictionary.

　① contribution 　② distribution 　③ decision 　④ supply

(4) The house is large and expensive to (　　　).

　① compare 　② expand 　③ maintain 　④ reform

(5) Oh, no! I seem (　　　) my wallet.

　① forget 　② have forgotten 　③ to forget 　④ to have forgotten

Listening 英文を聞いて理解しよう【知識・技能】【思考力・判断力・表現力】 (共通テスト) 🔘60

Listen to the English and make the best choice to match the content. （4点）

　① The speaker likes the fish in the aquarium.

　② The speaker manages the aquarium.

　③ The speaker knows about an aquarium run by high school students.

Interaction 英文を聞いて会話を続けよう【知識・技能】【思考力・判断力・表現力】 スピーキング・トレーナー 🔘61

Listen to the English and respond to the remarks. （7点）

〔メモ　　　　　　　　　　　　　　　　　　　　　　　　　　　　　　　　〕

Hints
crowded (混雑した), inconvenient (不便な), nature (自然), the cost of living (生活費)

Production (Writing) 自分の考えを書いて伝えよう【思考力・判断力・表現力】

Write your answer to the following question. （9点）

Have you ever organized any event or festival?

Hints
Yes の場合は，企画・運営した行事などについて具体的に書きましょう。No の場合は，企画・運営してみたい行事などについて書きましょう。

Invigorating Our Local Community

　　Today, / there are many local communities / where the number of young people / has been decreasing. // **Meanwhile**, / in one survey, / about 70% of high school students answered / that they wanted to stay in / or keep in touch with their hometowns / after **graduation**. // Young people value local communities /
5　and can be helpful / for their **sustainability**. //

　　Even while in high school, / students can start contributing / in the following ways. // First, / they can use what they learn / at school / and **strive** to do / what they can do / to help. // Second, / their **participation** itself / can **stimulate** local people. //

10　Once John F. Kennedy, / the 35th U.S. president, / **declared** / in his **inaugural** address, / "Ask not what your country can do / for you. // Ask what you can do / for your country." // Now, / all we have to do / is keep learning and thinking about this: / What can we do / for our local communities? //

(144 words)

音読しよう

スピーキング・トレーナー

Practice 1 スラッシュ位置で文を区切って読んでみよう ☐
Practice 2 音声を聞きながら，音声のすぐ後を追って読んでみよう ☐
TRY! 1分20秒以内に本文全体を音読しよう ☐

Reading　本文の内容を読んで理解しよう【知識・技能】【思考力・判断力・表現力】

共通テスト　GTEC®

Make the correct choice to complete each sentence or answer each question. （各5点 [(3)は完答]）

(1) What does "value" mean in line 4? ☐
　　① appreciate　　　② expect　　　③ measure　　　④ refuse

(2) According to one survey, many high school students answered that ☐.
　　① they preferred leaving their hometowns to staying there
　　② they preferred staying in their hometowns to leaving there
　　③ they were not satisfied with their hometowns
　　④ they would not keep in touch with their hometowns

(3) Which of the following are true? (Choose two options. The order does not matter.)
　　☐ · ☐
　　① High school students can contribute to local communities by using what they learn at school.
　　② It is important to think about what we can do for our local communities.
　　③ John F. Kennedy said in his address, "Ask what your country can do for you."
　　④ The number of young people has been increasing all over Japan.
　　⑤ There are local communities where 70% of the young people have left their hometowns.

✎ Vocabulary & Grammar　重要表現や文法事項について理解しよう【知識】　英検® GTEC®

Make the correct choice to complete each sentence.　（各3点）

(1) The government has (　　　) its intention to reduce taxes.
　① contributed　　　② declared　　　③ invented　　　④ started

(2) We can (　　　) in touch with each other by email.
　① continue　　　② create　　　③ keep　　　④ make

(3) The company has succeeded because it (　　　) to constantly innovate.
　① leads　　　② refers　　　③ relates　　　④ strives

(4) That lecture really (　　　) me.
　① conveyed　　　② inspected　　　③ proposed　　　④ stimulated

(5) All you have to do is (　　　) this letter.
　① post　　　② posted　　　③ posting　　　④ to posting

🎧 Listening　英文を聞いて理解しよう【知識・技能】【思考力・判断力・表現力】　共通テスト ◎62

Listen to the English and make the best choice to match the content.　（4点）
　① The speaker wants to get a job in her hometown.
　② The speaker wants to go to high school in her hometown.
　③ The speaker wants to start a business in her hometown.

💬 Interaction　英文を聞いて会話を続けよう【知識・技能】【思考力・判断力・表現力】　スピーキング・トレーナー ◎63

Listen to the English and respond to the remark.　（7点）
　〔メモ　　　　　　　　　　　　　　　　　　　　　　　　　　　　　　　　　　　〕

🎙 **Hints**
　あなたの地元が力を入れていることを参考にして考えましょう。

✍ Production（Writing）　自分の考えを書いて伝えよう【思考力・判断力・表現力】

Write your answer to the following question.　（9点）

What do you want to do for your community?

🎙 **Hints**
　assist at a facility for the elderly (高齢者施設で支援する), clean-up activity (清掃活動), teach elementary and junior high school students (小中学生に教える)

Lesson 9

Invigorating Our Local Community

Part 4

教科書 p.144-145 / 50

Interviewer: Our school's light music club / **regularly** hosts **live** concerts / at a local shopping **mall**. // Everyone around here looks forward to it, / and many people come / each time. // Let's listen to what the club members have to say now. // ... Well, / why did you start such an activity? //

5 *Kumi:* We wanted a lot of people / to listen to our music / because the **audience** in school events / is **mostly limited** / to friends and family. //

Interviewer: Have you found anything / through this activity? //

Taro: Yes! // At the first concert, / we were surprised / to find / so many people were interested / in high school students' activities. // We couldn't have 10 noticed this / if we had played / only at school. //

Interviewer: What do you want to do / in the future? //

Vivian: When I go back / to my home country, / I'd like to play music together / with the local people. //

Interviewer: Thank you so much / for your time. //

(143 words)

音読しよう 🔊))📖　　　　　　　　　　　　　　　　　　　　スピーキング・トレーナー

Practice 1 スラッシュ位置で文を区切って読んでみよう ☐
Practice 2 音声を聞きながら，音声のすぐ後を追って読んでみよう ☐
TRY! 1分20秒以内に本文全体を音読しよう ☐

📖 Reading　本文の内容を読んで理解しよう【知識・技能】【思考力・判断力・表現力】　　共通テスト

Make the correct choice to complete each sentence or answer each question. ((1)は7点,(2)は8点)

(1) The light music club started live concerts at a local shopping mall because ☐.
　① many people were interested in high school students' activities
　② the club members wanted more people other than their friends and family to listen to their music
　③ the club members wanted to play music together with the local people
　④ the local people asked the club members to host live concerts

(2) Which of the following is true? ☐
　① After returning to her home country, Vivian wants to be a musician.
　② The audience at the live concerts at a shopping mall was mostly friends and family.
　③ The light music club regularly hosts live concerts at school.
　④ The local people look forward to listening to the light music club's music.

Vocabulary & Grammar　重要表現や文法事項について理解しよう【知識】　英検®　GTEC®

Make the correct choice to complete each sentence.　(各3点)

(1)　The (　　　) at the rock concert was very loud.

　① audience　　　② character　　　③ individual　　　④ viewer

(2)　It's important to exercise (　　　) to keep in shape.

　① mainly　　　② naturally　　　③ rarely　　　④ regularly

(3)　Many cities compete to (　　　) the Olympics.

　① host　　　② rely　　　③ take　　　④ unite

(4)　The influence of the storm was not (　　　) to the area.

　① completed　　　② limited　　　③ surprised　　　④ treated

(5)　If you tried harder, you (　　　) in business.

　① could have made it　　　　　② could make it

　③ had made it　　　　　④ have made it

🎧 Listening　英文を聞いて理解しよう【知識・技能】【思考力・判断力・表現力】　共通テスト　💿64

Listen to the English and make the best choice to match the content.　(4点)

　① The speaker belongs to the light music club.

　② The speaker performs at the school festival.

　③ The speaker will listen to the performance by the light music club.

💬 Interaction　英文を聞いて会話を続けよう【知識・技能】【思考力・判断力・表現力】　スピーキング・トレーナー　💿65

Listen to the English and respond to the remark.　(7点)

〔メ モ　　　　　　　　　　　　　　　　　　　　　　　　　　　　　　　〕

🎧**Hints**
brass band (吹奏楽), calligraphy (書道), dance performance (ダンスパフォーマンス), photo contest (写真コンテスト)

🖊 Production (Writing)　自分の考えを書いて伝えよう【思考力・判断力・表現力】

Write your answer to the following question.　(9点)

What do you want to do in the future?

🎧**Hints**
将来の夢や就きたい職業などについて書きましょう。

Doing something / that harms animals / or their **habitats** / is NOT allowed / on our site. // You are searching for posts / that may **promote harmful behavior** / toward animals or the environment. //

Kumi: Hey, / I need your help! //

5 *David:* Hi, / Kumi. // What's wrong? //

Kumi: I wanted to see some photos / of animals / on social media. // Then, / this **pop-up** message appeared. // What's this? //

David: Let me see. // "... may promote harmful behavior / toward animals or the environment"?! // Well, / what were you doing / when it appeared? //

10 *Kumi:* Nothing special. //

David: But / ... it seems / that you did something / that might hurt animals. //

Kumi: Never would I think of doing something / like that. // I just don't understand / why I got this message. //

David: Hmm ... // What search words / did you use? //

15 *Kumi:* "Koala**selfie**." //

David: Um ... // Sorry, / I have no idea. // You'd better **click** / on the "Learn More" **link** / for more information. //

(132 words)

🔊) 音読しよう 📖 〜〜〜〜〜〜〜〜〜〜〜〜〜〜〜〜 スピーキング・トレーナー

Practice 1 スラッシュ位置で文を区切って読んでみよう ☐

Practice 2 音声を聞きながら，音声のすぐ後を追って読んでみよう ☐

TRY! 1分15秒以内に本文全体を音読しよう ☐

📖 **Reading** 本文の内容を読んで理解しよう【知識・技能】【思考力・判断力・表現力】 共通テスト GTEC®

Make the correct choice to complete each sentence or answer each question. （各5点）

(1) What does "promote" mean in line 2? ☐

　　① discourage　　　② encourage　　　③ operate　　　④ prevent

(2) Kumi asked David for help because a warning message popped up when ☐.

　　① she was searching for pictures of animals on social media

　　② she was showing her new smartphone to David

　　③ she was taking photos of animals

　　④ she was trying to post a photo with a koala

(3) You have learned that ☐.

　　① David searched for some pictures on social media

　　② David didn't know why Kumi got the message

　　③ Kumi clicked on the "Learn More" link

　　④ Kumi doesn't like animals

Vocabulary & Grammar　重要表現や文法事項について理解しよう【知識】　英検® GTEC®

Make the correct choice to complete each sentence.　（各3点）

(1)　The panda's natural (　　　) is in a bamboo forest.
　　① country　　　　② donation　　　　③ habitat　　　　④ landmark

(2)　To what degree does television influence the (　　　) of children?
　　① behavior　　　　② distance　　　　③ impact　　　　④ position

(3)　It's cold.　You (　　　) wear a coat at once.
　　① are going to　　② had better　　　③ had to　　　　④ must not

(4)　Some of these ingredients may be (　　　) to animals.
　　① beautiful　　　　② cheerful　　　　③ harmful　　　　④ peaceful

(5)　(　　　) the first page of the book when I became tired of reading it.
　　① Hardly had I read　② Hardly I had read　③ Had I hardly read　④ Had I read hardly

Listening　英文を聞いて理解しよう【知識・技能】【思考力・判断力・表現力】　共通テスト　🔘66

Listen to the English and make the best choice to match the content.　（4点）
　　① The speaker likes taking pictures.
　　② The speaker posts photos on social media.
　　③ The speaker searches for photos and posts on social media.

Interaction　英文を聞いて会話を続けよう【知識・技能】【思考力・判断力・表現力】　スピーキング・トレーナー　🔘67

Listen to the English and respond to the last remark.　（7点）
　　〔メ モ　　　　　　　　　　　　　　　　　　　　　　　　　　　　　　〕

🌡**Hints**
　I like ... や My favorite animal is ... などの表現を使って，好きな動物を紹介しましょう。

Production（Writing）　自分の考えを書いて伝えよう【思考力・判断力・表現力】

Write your answer to the following question.　（9点）
Zoos are popular, but some people think zoos are cruel to animals.　What do you think about zoos?

🌡**Hints**
　amuse (…を楽しませる)，separate an animal from its natural habitat (動物を自然生息地から引き離す)

What do people like to do / when they are on vacation? // These days, / many people enjoy **interacting** / with animals / by participating in **wildlife tourism**. // Some people can hold a koala or a **sloth** / in their arms, / while others can swim / with dolphins. // During these experiences, / they often take selfies /
5 with the animals / and post the photos / online. //

This kind of tourism / has become extremely popular / as social media have **prevailed** / on the Internet. // As you may guess, / posting selfies with the animals / on social media / encourages wildlife tourism. // Site visitors may be inspired / to do the same. //

10 Now, / take a moment / to think about the friendly animals / that meet with the tourists. // Actually, / there is something / hidden on the **underside** / of wildlife tourism. // Having suffered great **agonies** / caused by **human beings**, / some animals are in terrible health. //

(137 words)

音読しよう   スピーキング・トレーナー

Practice 1 スラッシュ位置で文を区切って読んでみよう ☐
Practice 2 音声を聞きながら，音声のすぐ後を追って読んでみよう ☐
TRY! 1分15秒以内に本文全体を音読しよう ☐

Reading 本文の内容を読んで理解しよう【知識・技能】【思考力・判断力・表現力】   共通テスト

Make the correct choice to complete each sentence or answer each question. (各5点)

(1) Which of the following is **not** written as an example of wildlife tourism? ☐
　① Going on vacation.　　　　② Holding a koala.
　③ Holding a sloth.　　　　④ Swimming with dolphins.

(2) Wildlife tourism has become popular because ☐ .
　① animals like to interact with human beings
　② more and more people are going on vacation
　③ most people like animals
　④ posts of selfies with animals on social media inspire people to interact with animals

(3) What does the last paragraph try to tell the readers? ☐
　① Be careful of animals since they are not always friendly.
　② How cute wild animals are.
　③ Human beings are having negative impacts on animals through wildlife tourism.
　④ Using social media too much can affect your health.

Vocabulary & Grammar　重要表現や文法事項について理解しよう【知識】　英検® GTEC®

Make the correct choice to complete each sentence.　（各3点）

(1) Lucy (　　　) well with other children in the class.
　① contrasts　　　② interacts　　　③ participates　　　④ reflects

(2) I'd like to visit France in this summer (　　　).
　① absence　　　② break　　　③ vacation　　　④ weekend

(3) The team was (　　　) by the coach's words.
　① advised　　　② inspired　　　③ reminded　　　④ struggled

(4) He was in (　　　) because of his constant back pain.
　① agony　　　② comfort　　　③ disappointment　　　④ pleasure

(5) (　　　) in Hawaii for a long time, he is used to the tropical climate.
　① Had lived　　　② Having lived　　　③ In living　　　④ Lived

Listening　英文を聞いて理解しよう【知識・技能】【思考力・判断力・表現力】　共通テスト 💿 68

Listen to the English and make the best choice to match the content.　（4点）
　① The speaker has no plan for this summer.
　② The speaker went to Australia this summer.
　③ The speaker will see koalas at a zoo in Australia.

Interaction　英文を聞いて会話を続けよう【知識・技能】【思考力・判断力・表現力】　スピーキング・トレーナー 💿 69

Listen to the English and respond to the remark.　（7点）
　〔メモ　　　　　　　　　　　　　　　　　　　　　　　　　　　　　　　　　　〕
　🔑 **Hints**
　それぞれのメリット・デメリットを考えましょう。

Production（Writing）　自分の考えを書いて伝えよう【思考力・判断力・表現力】

Write your answer to the following question.　（9点）
If you are going on a wildlife tourism trip, what kind of wildlife would you like to see?
Why?

　🔑 **Hints**
　crane (鶴), koala (コアラ), polar bear (北極グマ), whale (クジラ)

In wildlife tourism, / tourists can enjoy encounters / with attractive animals. // For example, / there are adult tigers / that are gentle enough / for people / to touch, / and there are tiger **cubs** / that tourists can **snuggle** up with. // In fact, / the adult tigers may be **declawed**, / given some special **drug**, / or both. // The
5 cubs are taken from their mothers / just days after birth / so that the mothers can have new babies / as soon as possible. //

Sloths are popular animals / for selfies. // They naturally live / in tropical forests. // However, / some sloths are taken **illegally** / from **jungles** / for business purposes. // Once they are caught / and kept in a **cage**, / they often die / within weeks. //

10 Most of the tourists don't know these facts. // Probably, / the animals' behavior appears / to them / as if the animals were also having fun / with them. // Sadly, / this human view may help promote the business. //

(143 words)

🔊)) **音読しよう** 📖 ～～～～～～～～～～～ スピーキング・トレーナー

Practice 1 スラッシュ位置で文を区切って読んでみよう ☐
Practice 2 音声を聞きながら，音声のすぐ後を追って読んでみよう ☐
TRY! 1分20秒以内に本文全体を音読しよう ☐

📖 **Reading** 本文の内容を読んで理解しよう【知識・技能】【思考力・判断力・表現力】 （共通テスト）

Make the correct choice to complete each sentence or answer each question. （各5点）

(1) Tiger cubs are taken from their mothers just days after birth because ☐.
① the cubs become more friendly toward people ② the cubs often die in a cage
③ the mothers can have more babies soon ④ the mothers neglect to raise their cubs

(2) Which of the following is **not** true? ☐
① The adult tigers may be given some special drug.
② Tourists can snuggle up with tiger cubs.
③ Tigers naturally live in tropical forests.
④ Some sloths are taken illegally from jungles for business purposes.

(3) Most of the tourists don't know that ☐.
① animals are having fun with them
② sloths are popular animals for selfies
③ they can enjoy encounters with animals
④ wildlife tourism has some negative impacts on the animals

Goals

🔊 意味の区切りを理解してスムーズに音読することができる。　📖 ワイルドライフツーリズムに関する英文を読んで概要や要点をとらえることができる。
📝 文脈を理解して適切な語句を用いて英文を完成することができる。　🎧 平易な英語で話される短い英文を聞いて必要な情報を聞き取ることができる。
💬 動物について簡単な語句を用いて情報や考えを伝えることができる。　✍ ワイルドライフツーリズムについて簡単な語句を用いて考えを表現することができる。

Vocabulary & Grammar 　重要表現や文法事項について理解しよう【知識】　英検® GTEC®

Make the correct choice to complete each sentence. （各3点）

(1) Our new season's jackets are more (　　　) than last year's.
　① attractive　　　② lucky　　　③ national　　　④ polite

(2) The (　　　) was found to cause serious side effects.
　① drug　　　② experience　　　③ fact　　　④ history

(3) Try to finish the job as soon (　　　).
　① as can　　　② as possible　　　③ as you possible　　　④ than possible

(4) Police said the man entered the country (　　　) by using a fake passport.
　① currently　　　② illegally　　　③ silently　　　④ traditionally

(5) He glared at her as if she (　　　) something wrong.
　① do　　　② does　　　③ had done　　　④ has done

Listening 　英文を聞いて理解しよう【知識・技能】【思考力・判断力・表現力】　共通テスト 💿70

Listen to the English and make the best choice to match the content. （4点）
　① The speaker couldn't see sea turtles.
　② The speaker is from Okinawa Prefecture.
　③ The speaker took part in wildlife tourism in Okinawa.

Interaction 　英文を聞いて会話を続けよう【知識・技能】【思考力・判断力・表現力】　スピーキング・トレーナー 💿71

Listen to the English and respond to the last remark. （7点）
〔メモ　　　　　　　　　　　　　　　　　　　　　　　　　　　　　　　　　　　　〕

🔑**Hints**
alpaca (アルパカ)，lion (ライオン)，koala (コアラ)，pony (ポニー)

Production (Writing) 　自分の考えを書いて伝えよう【思考力・判断力・表現力】

Write your answer to the following question. （9点）
What do you think are advantages of wildlife tourism?

🔑**Hints**
「Did You Know? ② ワイルドライフツーリズムの裏側」（教科書 p. 162-163）の内容も参考にして書きましょう。

Lesson 10 The Underside of Wildlife Tourism

Wildlife tourism has caused some serious problems. // Tourists and social media / have **responsibility** for this. // **Whoever** enjoys contact with animals / on vacation / just feels happy / to be with them. // Those people never think / that their behaviors might hurt animals and the **ecosystem**. // **Moreover**, /
5 seeing the posted selfies / on social media, / the site visitors may hope / to have the same experiences. //

Recently, / social media's role / in the problem / has been recognized. // A social media site started / to show a pop-up warning / when its users search, / using **hashtags** / like "#slothselfie" and "#koalaselfie." //

10 Today, / social media are such **prevailing** communication tools / that they can have a great impact anywhere. // Even the **single** act / of posting a photo / can lead to animal **abuse**. // Next time you take and post photos, / think about how your photos might affect others. //

(134 words)

🔊)) 音読しよう 📖 ～～～～～～～～ スピーキング・トレーナー

Practice 1 スラッシュ位置で文を区切って読んでみよう ☐
Practice 2 音声を聞きながら，音声のすぐ後を追って読んでみよう ☐
TRY! 1分15秒以内に本文全体を音読しよう ☐

📖 Reading　本文の内容を読んで理解しよう【知識・技能】【思考力・判断力・表現力】　(共通テスト)

Make the correct choice to complete each sentence or answer each question. ((1)は7点, (2)は8点)

(1) Social media ☐ .

   ① don't have responsibility for serious problems caused by wildlife tourism

   ② never encourage people to take part in wildlife tourism

   ③ started a campaign to promote wildlife tourism all over the world

   ④ started to show a warning message when their users use words related to animal abuse

(2) Which of the following is true? ☐

   ① A social media site is encouraging its users to use hashtags.

   ② People who enjoy contact with animals always think that they might hurt animals and the ecosystem.

   ③ Social media can have a great impact on wildlife tourism.

   ④ Wildlife tourism is making good use of social media to protect the environment.

Vocabulary & Grammar 重要表現や文法事項について理解しよう【知識】 英検® GTEC®

Make the correct choice to complete each sentence. （各3点）

(1) All drivers have (　　　) for traffic safety.
① ability　　　② chemistry　　　③ difficulty　　　④ responsibility

(2) I learned wolves are very important to the (　　　).
① attitude　　　② behavior　　　③ ecosystem　　　④ source

(3) Vivian remained silent. She didn't say a (　　　) word.
① major　　　② single　　　③ total　　　④ whole

(4) He is a quick worker, and (　　　), he is careful.
① instead　　　② moreover　　　③ so　　　④ therefore

(5) (　　　) telephones, tell them I'm out.
① Whatever　　　② Whenever　　　③ Whichever　　　④ Whoever

Listening 英文を聞いて理解しよう【知識・技能】【思考力・判断力・表現力】 共通テスト 72

Listen to the English and make the best choice to match the content. （4点）
① Koalas feel stressed when people hold them.
② People can hold koalas in all states in Australia.
③ The speaker lives in Australia.

Interaction 英文を聞いて会話を続けよう【知識・技能】【思考力・判断力・表現力】 スピーキング・トレーナー 73

Listen to the English and respond to the last remark. （7点）
〔メモ　　　　　　　　　　　　　　　　　　　　　　　　　　　　　　　　　　　　　〕

Hints
SNS を使う際に注意していることを話しましょう。

Production (Writing) 自分の考えを書いて伝えよう【思考力・判断力・表現力】

Write your answer to the following question. （9点）
Write about a human behavior that harms animals.

Hints
global warming (地球温暖化), microplastic pollution (マイクロプラスチック汚染)

I remember well the **wooden** case / **fastened** to the wall / on the stair **landing**. // The **receiver hung** / on the side of the box. // I even remember the number / —— 105. // I was too little / to reach the telephone, / but used to listen **eagerly** / when my mother talked to it. // Once / she **lifted** me up / to speak to my father, /

5 who was away / on business. // Magic! //

Then / I discovered / that somewhere inside that wonderful **device** / lived an amazing person / —— her name was "Information Please" / and there was nothing / she did not know. //

My mother could ask her / for anybody's number; / when our clock ran down, /

10 Information Please immediately **supplied** the correct time. //

(110 words)

◁)) 音読しよう 📖 ～～～～～～～～～～～～ スピーキング・トレーナー

Practice 1 スラッシュ位置で文を区切って読んでみよう ☐
Practice 2 音声を聞きながら，音声のすぐ後を追って読んでみよう ☐
TRY! 1分以内に本文全体を音読しよう ☐

📖 Reading 本文の内容を読んで理解しよう【知識・技能】【思考力・判断力・表現力】 （共通テスト）

Make the correct choice to answer each question. ((1)は7点, (2)は8点)
(1) Which of the following is true about the telephone that the author's family had? ☐
 ① The author was not allowed to use it because he was so young.
 ② The author couldn't reach it because he was too little.
 ③ It was fastened to the wall, but the author could reach it.
 ④ It was the wooden case that stood on the stair landing.
(2) What seemed like "magic" to the author? ☐
 ① Being lifted up by his mother.
 ② Discovering that a person named "Information Please" lived inside the telephone.
 ③ Listening when his mother talked on the telephone.
 ④ Speaking to his father, who was away on business.

✒ Vocabulary 重要表現について理解しよう【知識】 英検® GTEC®

Make the correct choice to complete each sentence. （各5点）
(1) Many stars are ( ) far away from the earth to be seen with the naked eye.
 ① as ② so ③ too ④ very
(2) She'll be back next week —— she's away ( ) business now.
 ① by ② for ③ in ④ on
(3) Do you think scientists will ( ) a planet similar to earth?
 ① destroy ② discover ③ look ④ see

My first personal experience / with this woman-in-the-receiver / came one day / while my mother was visiting a neighbor. // **Amusing** myself / with a **hammer**, / I hit my finger. // The pain was terrible, / but there didn't seem to be much use crying / because there was no one home / to hear me. // I
5 walked around the house / **sucking** my finger, / finally arriving at the landing. // The telephone! // Quickly / I ran for the **footstool** / and took it / to the landing. // Climbing up, / I took the receiver / and held it to my ear. // "Information Please," / I said into the **mouthpiece** / just above my head. //

A click or two, / and a small, clear voice / spoke into my ear. //
10 "Information." //

"I hurt my fingerrrrr ——" / I cried into the phone. // The tears began running down, / now that I had an audience. //

"Isn't your mother home?" / came the question. //

"Nobody's home / but me," / I said. //
15 "Are you **bleeding**?" //

"No," / I replied. // "I hit it / with the hammer / and it hurts." //

"Can you open your **icebox**?" / she asked. // I said / I could. //

"Then / break off a little piece of ice / and hold it / on your finger. // That will stop the hurt. // Be careful / when you use the ice pick," / she **warned**. // "And
20 don't cry. // You'll be all right." //

(207 words)

音読しよう

スピーキング・トレーナー

Practice 1 スラッシュ位置で文を区切って読んでみよう ☐
Practice 2 音声を聞きながら，音声のすぐ後を追って読んでみよう ☐
TRY! 1分50秒以内に本文全体を音読しよう ☐

Make the correct choice to complete each sentence. （各5点）

(1) One day, the author hit his finger with a hammer. The pain was terrible, ____.

  ① and he cried so that somebody would come to help him

  ② and he cried so that somebody would notice him

  ③ but he didn't cry because he was patient

  ④ but he didn't cry because there was no one home to hear him

(2) The author asked Information Please for help because he knew that ____.

  ① she would come to help him

  ② she would help him somehow

  ③ she would keep his injury secret

  ④ she would let him cry as much as he wanted

(3) The last sentence "You'll be all right." is closest in meaning to "____"

  ① Be brave. You're a good boy.

  ② Give it a try. It won't hurt you.

  ③ That will stop bleeding.

  ④ The hurt will stop soon.

Make the correct choice to complete each sentence. （各3点）

(1) (   ) to be something wrong with the engine.

  ① It looks   ② It seems   ③ There looks   ④ There seems

(2) There is no (   ) studying for an exam at the last minute.

  ① purpose   ② result   ③ use   ④ way

(3) (   ) the children have left home, we can move to a smaller house.

  ① Although   ② Even if   ③ If only   ④ Now that

(4) I (   ) him not to trust John.

  ① declared   ② discussed   ③ suggested   ④ warned

(5) Could you break (   ) another bit of chocolate for me?

  ① down   ② off   ③ on   ④ up

Information Please

After that, / I called Information Please / for everything. // I asked for help / with my **geography** / and she told me / where Philadelphia was, / and the Orinoco / —— the river / I was going to **explore** / when I grew up. // She helped me / with my **arithmetic**, / and she told me / that a pet **chipmunk** / —— I had caught him / in the

5 park / just the day before / —— would eat fruit and nuts. //

And / there was the time / that our pet **canary** died. // I called Information Please / and told her the sad story. // She listened, / and then said the usual things / **grown-ups** say / to **soothe** a child. // But I did not feel better: / why should birds sing so beautifully / and bring joy / to whole families, / only to end as a **heap** of **feathers** / feet

10 up, / on the bottom of a cage? //

She must have sensed my deep **concern**, / for she said quietly, / "Paul, / always remember / that there are other worlds / to sing in." //

Somehow / I felt better. //

(160 words)

音読しよう   スピーキング・トレーナー

Practice 1 スラッシュ位置で文を区切って読んでみよう ☐
Practice 2 音声を聞きながら，音声のすぐ後を追って読んでみよう ☐
TRY! 1分25秒以内に本文全体を音読しよう ☐

📖 Reading 本文の内容を読んで理解しよう【知識・技能】【思考力・判断力・表現力】   (共通テスト)

Make the correct choice to complete each sentence.   ((1)は7点，(2)は8点)
(1) Judging from the first paragraph, the author was ☐ when he was a child.
　① cheerful and very selfish　　　　② full of energy and very active
　③ sensitive and very nervous　　　④ very playful and often caused troubles
(2) The author wanted to know ☐.
　① why birds bring joy to us all　　② why birds should be kept in cages
　③ why birds should die　　　　　　④ why birds sing so beautifully

🔖 Vocabulary 重要表現について理解しよう【知識】   (英検®) (GTEC®)

Make the correct choice to complete each sentence.   (各5点)
(1) Some people think it's wrong to spend much money on (　　　) space.
　① developing　　② discovering　　③ exploring　　④ regarding
(2) The baby was crying, so I tried to (　　　) her by singing to her.
　① hold　　　　② hug　　　　③ soothe　　　④ wake
(3) He bought the software, (　　　) to discover that it wouldn't work on his computer.
　① in order　　② just　　③ only　　④ so as

Information Please

Optional
Lesson 2

Part 4
教科書 p.173-174 / 30

Another day / I was at the telephone. // "Information," / said the now familiar voice. //

"How do you spell **fix**?" / I asked. //

"Fix something? // F-I-X." //

5 　At that **instant** / my sister, / trying to **scare** me, / jumped off the stairs at me. // I fell off the footstool, / pulling the receiver / out of the box. // We were both **terrified** / —— Information Please was no longer there, / and I was not at all sure / that I hadn't hurt her / when I pulled the receiver out. //

　Minutes later / there was a man at the door. // "I'm a telephone 10 **repairman**. // I was working down the street / and the **operator** said / there might be some trouble / at this number." // He reached for the receiver / in my hand. // "What happened?" //

I told him. //

"Well, / we can fix that / in a minute or two." // He opened the telephone 15 box, / did some **repair** work, / and then spoke into the phone. // "Hi, / this is Pete. // Everything's under control / at 105. // The kid's sister scared him / and he pulled the **cord** / out of the box." //

　He hung up, / smiled, / gave me a **pat** on the head / and walked out of the door. //

(187 words)

Practice 1 スラッシュ位置で文を区切って読んでみよう ☐
Practice 2 音声を聞きながら，音声のすぐ後を追って読んでみよう ☐
TRY! 1分40秒以内に本文全体を音読しよう ☐

スピーキング・トレーナー

Reading 本文の内容を読んで理解しよう【知識・技能】【思考力・判断力・表現力】 共通テスト

Make the correct choice to complete each sentence or answer each question.

((1)は 7 点，(2)は完答 8 点)

(1) When the author pulled the receiver out of the box, he thought that ☐.

　① he could not have hurt Information Please

　② he had not hurt Information Please

　③ he might have hurt Information Please

　④ he must have hurt Information Please

(2) Put the following events (①〜④) into the order in which they happened.

　☐ → ☐ → ☐ → ☐

　① Information Please telephoned the repairman to say that there might be some trouble at 105.

　② The author told the repairman what had happened.

　③ The repairman appeared at the door.

　④ The repairman telephoned Information Please to say that he had finished his work.

Vocabulary 重要表現について理解しよう【知識】 英検® GTEC®

Make the correct choice to complete each sentence. (各 3 点)

(1) The teacher ( ) the student out of class to speak to him privately.

　① moved　　　② pulled　　　③ put　　　④ turned

(2) We can't give ( ) answers to such difficult questions.

　① fast　　　② former　　　③ initial　　　④ instant

(3) It seems that the spread of the disease is now ( ) control.

　① below　　　② in　　　③ under　　　④ with

(4) The moment I hung ( ) the telephone, I realized that I had forgotten to say something.

　① at　　　② in　　　③ on　　　④ up

(5) Laura's father came home and ( ) her a big hug.

　① gave　　　② had　　　③ made　　　④ took

Optional Lesson 2　**89**

All this took place / in a small town / in the Pacific Northwest. // Then, / when I was nine years old, / we moved / across the country to Boston / —— and I missed Information Please / very much. // She **belonged** in that old wooden box back home, / and I somehow never thought of trying the tall, **skinny** new phone / that sat on a

5 small table / in the hall. //

Yet, / as I grew into my **teens**, / the memories of those **childhood** conversations / never really left me; / often in moments of doubt and worry / I would recall the serene sense of security / I had / when I knew / that I could call Information Please / and get the right answer. // I appreciated now / how patient, understanding and kind she was /

10 to have wasted her time / on a little boy. //

(130 words)

音読しよう 📖 ─────────────── スピーキング・トレーナー

Practice 1 スラッシュ位置で文を区切って読んでみよう ☐

Practice 2 音声を聞きながら，音声のすぐ後を追って読んでみよう ☐

TRY! 1分10秒以内に本文全体を音読しよう ☐

📖 Reading 本文の内容を読んで理解しよう【知識・技能】【思考力・判断力・表現力】 （共通テスト）

Make the correct choice to complete each sentence or answer each question. （(1)は7点, (2)は8点）

(1) The author didn't telephone Information Please from Boston. That was because ☐.
　① he didn't feel sad that Information Please was not with him anymore
　② he didn't know how to make a long-distance call
　③ he felt that Information Please lived in the old wooden box back home, not in the skinny new phone on a small table
　④ he no longer lived in the same town as Information Please did

(2) Which of the following is **not** true? ☐
　① As a teenager, the author often had doubt and worry.
　② The author felt sorry that he had made Information Please waste her time.
　③ The author never forgot those childhood conversations with Information Please.
　④ The author realized how patient, understanding and kind Information Please was.

🗂 Vocabulary 重要表現について理解しよう【知識】 （英検®）（GTEC®）

Make the correct choice to complete each sentence. （各5点）

(1) I'll (　　) you when you go away.
　① miss　　　　　② recognize　　　　③ remember　　　④ thank

(2) Lisa (　　) to the basketball team.
　① belongs　　　② decides　　　　③ enables　　　④ proves

(3) Don't leave the light on. You're (　　) electricity.
　① spending　　② supplying　　　③ treating　　　④ wasting

A few years later, / on my way west to college, / my plane landed in Seattle. // I had about half an hour / before my plane left, / and I spent 15 minutes or so / on the phone / with my sister, / who had a happy marriage there now. // Then, / really without thinking / what I was doing, / I **dialed** my
5 hometown operator / and said, / "Information Please." //

Miraculously, / I heard again the small, clear voice / I knew so well: / "Information." //

I hadn't planned this, / but I heard myself saying, / "Could you tell me, / please, / how to spell the word 'fix'?" //

10 There was a long pause. // Then / came the softly spoken answer. // "I guess," / said Information Please, / "that your finger must be all right / by now." //

I laughed. // "So / it's really still you. // I wonder / if you have any idea / how much you meant to me / during all that time ..." //

"I wonder," / she replied, / "if you know / how much you meant to me? // I
15 never had any children, / and I used to look forward to your calls. // **Silly**, / wasn't it?" //

It didn't seem silly, / but I didn't say so. // Instead / I told her / how often I had thought of her / over the years, / and I asked / if I could call her again / when I came back / to visit my sister / after the first **semester** was over. //

20 "Please do. // Just ask for Sally." //

"Goodbye, / Sally." // It sounded strange / for Information Please to have a name. // "If I run into any chipmunks, / I'll tell them / to eat fruit and nuts." //

"Do that," / she said. // "And / I expect / one of these days / you'll visit the Orinoco. // Well, / goodbye." //

(269 words)

音読しよう

スピーキング・トレーナー

Practice 1 スラッシュ位置で文を区切って読んでみよう ☐
Practice 2 音声を聞きながら，音声のすぐ後を追って読んでみよう ☐
TRY! 2分25秒以内に本文全体を音読しよう ☐

Make the correct choice to complete each sentence or answer each question. （各5点）

(1) The author was in Seattle on his way west to college. What did he do? ☐

　① He dialed his hometown operator in order to talk to Information Please.

　② He telephoned his sister to hear about Information Please.

　③ He wanted to hear Information Please's voice, so he dialed his hometown operator.

　④ Without intention to do so, he dialed his hometown operator.

(2) Information Please brought Paul back into her mind ☐

　① after he said, "Could you tell me, please, how to spell the word 'fix'?"

　② after she said, "I guess that your finger must be all right by now."

　③ soon after he said "Information Please."

　④ soon after she said "Information."

(3) Which of the following is **not** true? ☐

　① Information Please and the author meant a lot to each other.

　② Information Please was tired of waiting for the author's call.

　③ The author and Information Please promised to talk on the phone again.

　④ The author and Information Please remembered each of their conversations.

Make the correct choice to complete each sentence. （各3点）

(1) I was already (　　　) my way to school when I realized I had forgotten my box lunch.

　① by　　　　　　② from　　　　　　③ on　　　　　　④ to

(2) You have no (　　　) how difficult it was to find a time that suited everybody.

　① idea　　　　　② image　　　　　③ imagination　　④ impression

(3) Karen trained day and night —— winning the gold medal (　　　) everything to her.

　① got　　　　　　② made　　　　　③ meant　　　　　④ required

(4) The kids are (　　　) forward to their vacation. They have never been to California before.

　① looking　　　　② running　　　　③ seeing　　　　④ waiting

(5) I'm glad I (　　　) into you. I wanted to ask you about tomorrow's history test.

　① came　　　　　② met　　　　　　③ ran　　　　　　④ went

Just three months later / I was back again / at the Seattle airport. // A different voice answered, / "Information," / and I asked for Sally. //

"Are you a friend?" //

"Yes," / I said. // "An old friend." //

5   "Then / I'm sorry / to have to tell you. // Sally had only been working **part-time** / in the last few years / because she was ill. // She died five weeks ago." // But before I could hang up, / she said, / "Wait a minute. // Did you say / your name was Willard?" //

"Yes." //

"Well, / Sally left a message / for you. // She wrote it down." //

10   "What was it?" / I asked, / almost knowing in advance / what it would be. //

"Here it is, / I'll read it / —— 'Tell him / I still say / there are other worlds / to sing in. // He'll know / what I mean.' " //

I thanked her / and hung up. // I did know / what Sally meant. //

(139 words)

音読しよう

スピーキング・トレーナー

Practice 1 スラッシュ位置で文を区切って読んでみよう ☐
Practice 2 音声を聞きながら，音声のすぐ後を追って読んでみよう ☐
TRY! 1分15秒以内に本文全体を音読しよう ☐

Reading
本文の内容を読んで理解しよう【知識・技能】【思考力・判断力・表現力】   共通テスト

Make the correct choice to complete each sentence or answer each question. ((1)は7点, (2)は8点)

(1) When a different voice answered, "Information," the author most likely said "[＿＿]"
  ① This is Paul. Can I speak to Sally?   ② This is Paul. I am an old friend of Sally's.
  ③ This is Willard. Can I ask Sally to call me back later?
  ④ This is Willard. Can I speak to Sally?

(2) Which of the following is true? [＿＿]
  ① Sally died five weeks after she last talked to the author on the telephone.
  ② The author had no idea what Sally had written down as a message to him.
  ③ The author thanked Sally and hung up.
  ④ The author understood the meaning of Sally's message.

Vocabulary
重要表現について理解しよう【知識】   英検®   GTEC®

Make the correct choice to complete each sentence. (各5点)

(1) He has been (   ) in bed for a week.
  ① bad   ② healthy   ③ ill   ④ sickness

(2) If you want to reserve seats, you will have to pay (   ).
  ① in advance   ② in charge   ③ in front   ④ in return

(3) You didn't understand the whole point. That wasn't (   ).
  ① my means   ② what I meant   ③ what you meant   ④ your meaning

Naomi Osaka's Interview after the 2018 U.S. Open

教科書 p. 181 　　／ 15

> *In the U.S. Open finals, | Naomi beat Serena Williams, | the **former** world number one player. || She was interviewed | after the match. ||*

Naomi: I know / that everyone was cheering / for Serena. //　I'm sorry / our final match had to end / like this. //　I just wanna say thank you / for watching the

5　match. //　Thank you. //

Interviewer: The first Japanese player, / **male** or female, / from your country / in history / to win a Grand Slam final. //

Naomi: My dream was / to play with Serena / in the U.S. Open finals. //　So / I'm really glad / that I was able to do that, / and I'm really **grateful** / I was able to

10　play with her. //　Thank you! //

(105 words)

🔊)) **音読しよう** 📖　　　　　　　　　　　　　　　　　　　スピーキング・トレーナー

Practice 1　スラッシュ位置で文を区切って読んでみよう ☐
Practice 2　音声を聞きながら，音声のすぐ後を追って読んでみよう ☐
TRY!　55秒以内に本文全体を音読しよう ☐

📖 Reading　本文の内容を読んで理解しよう【知識・技能】【思考力・判断力・表現力】　　　　(共通テスト)

Make the correct choice to complete each sentence or answer each question.　((1)は 7 点, (2)は 8 点)

(1)　Naomi apologized in the interview because she ☐ .

①　beat Serena Williams in the U.S. Open finals

②　couldn't make her dream come true

③　didn't win the tennis match even though everyone was supporting her

④　lost the final match with Serena Williams

(2)　Which of the following is true?　☐

①　Naomi became the first Japanese tennis player who won a Grand Slam final.

②　Naomi wasn't glad because no one was cheering for her.

③　Serena Williams became the world number one player after the 2018 U.S. Open finals.

④　To play with Naomi in the U.S. Open finals was Serena's dream.

Easy Banana **Muffin** Recipe //

Ingredients / for a **dozen** muffins //

📏× 1/3 butter   📏× 1/2 brown sugar   2 eggs

3 bananas   📏× 1/4 milk   📏× 2 **flour**

5   How to cook //

1. **Preheat** the **oven** / to 160℃. //

2. Put the butter and brown sugar / in a bowl, / and mix them together. //

3. Add eggs, / **mashed** bananas / and milk. //

4. Add the flour / to the bowl, / and mix all the ingredients. //

10 5. Put the **mixture** / in individual muffin cups. //

6. Bake the muffins / in the oven / for 20-25 minutes. //   Stop baking them / when their **surfaces** turn light brown. //

Comments

Vivian: **Incredible**. //   These muffins are SO good. //

15 Rachel: Easy to make! //   I made a dozen of them / with my kids. //   They liked them so much! //

(114 words)

🔊)) **音読しよう** 📖〜〜〜〜〜〜〜〜〜〜〜〜〜〜〜〜〜〜〜〜〜〜   **スピーキング・トレーナー**

Practice 1   スラッシュ位置で文を区切って読んでみよう ☐

Practice 2   音声を聞きながら，音声のすぐ後を追って読んでみよう ☐

TRY!   1分以内に本文全体を音読しよう ☐

📖 **Reading**   本文の内容を読んで理解しよう【知識・技能】【思考力・判断力・表現力】   (共通テスト)

Make the correct choice to complete each sentence or answer each question.   (各5点)

(1) How many muffins can you make with this recipe?   ☐

① 2   ② 3   ③ 12   ④ 20-25

(2) You need to ☐ just before adding flour to the bowl.

① add eggs, mashed bananas and milk   ② preheat the oven to 160℃

③ put the butter and brown sugar in a bowl   ④ put the mixture in individual muffin cups

(3) You have learned that ☐ .

① Rachel's children didn't like the muffins

② Vivian made the banana muffins with her children

③ you need to bake the muffins in the pan for 20-25 minutes

④ you need to stop baking the muffins when their surfaces turn light brown

A New Map Symbol

教科書 p. 183 　/ 15

Manabu: This is a new map symbol. //　It stands for a natural disaster **monument**. //

Vivian: Um, / why do we need a new symbol / now? //

Manabu: In recent years, / **torrential** rains have caused floods. //　Some areas have

5　suffered serious damage, / and people have lost their homes and families. //

Vivian: Ah! //　It sounds terrible. //

Manabu: I think so, / too. //　Anyway, / people in the past wanted their **descendants** / to remember their sad experiences. //　They **erected** monuments / which told / where past disasters had happened / and how much

10　damage / they had caused. //

Vivian: The Japanese government has used the **wisdom** / of people in the past / to create a new map symbol, / hasn't it? //

Manabu: That's right. //　The government did that / to warn residents / about the risks of disasters / in their neighborhoods. //

15　*Vivian:* That sounds like a great idea! //

(125 words)

音読しよう　スピーキング・トレーナー

Practice 1 スラッシュ位置で文を区切って読んでみよう ☐
Practice 2 音声を聞きながら，音声のすぐ後を追って読んでみよう ☐
TRY! 1分5秒以内に本文全体を音読しよう ☐

Reading 本文の内容を読んで理解しよう【知識・技能】【思考力・判断力・表現力】 　共通テスト

Make the correct choice to complete each sentence or answer each question. ((1)は7点, (2)は8点)

(1) People in the past erected monuments ☐.

　① to tell where future natural disasters are likely to happen

　② to tell where past disasters had happened and how much damage they had caused

　③ to tell where past evacuation sites used to be located

　④ to tell where people can hear the voices of natural disaster survivors

(2) Which of the following is true about the map symbol? ☐

　① It stands for a natural disaster monument.

　② People in the past created it.

　③ People in the past used the wisdom of the Japanese government to create it.

　④ The government created it to tell when natural disasters will happen.

Good evening. // This is our top story tonight. //

Today, / in Montreal, / one of the city's favorite stores / celebrated its 60th **anniversary**. // The store was opened / by a young immigrant / from Poland, / who arrived in Canada / in 1952. // This Pole was full of **motivation**, / and he wanted to

5　bring his love for bread / to his new home. // The local community welcomed him and his recipes. // His **bagels** have become very popular / in the city. //

To show its gratitude, / the store held a special event / for the local community. // The family-run business invited people / to come and learn / how to make its delicious bagels. // The event brought people / of different cultures

10　and **backgrounds** / together. // The owner hopes / that people from a lot of different backgrounds / share their love for bagels. //

(128 words)

🔊)) **音読しよう** 📖 ～～～～～～～～～　　　　　　　　スピーキング・トレーナー

Practice 1 スラッシュ位置で文を区切って読んでみよう ☐
Practice 2 音声を聞きながら，音声のすぐ後を追って読んでみよう ☐
TRY! 1分5秒以内に本文全体を音読しよう ☐

📖 **Reading** 本文の内容を読んで理解しよう【知識・技能】【思考力・判断力・表現力】　　共通テスト　GTEC®

Make the correct choice to complete each sentence or answer each question. (各5点)

(1) What does "gratitude" mean in line 7? ☐
　① happiness　　　② kindness　　　③ sadness　　　④ thanks

(2) A young immigrant from Poland ☐.
　① came to Canada to build a new house
　② opened his own store in Canada
　③ wanted to eat bagels at a favorite bagel store
　④ was full of depression

(3) Which of the following is true? ☐
　① The local people learned how to make delicious bagels at the event.
　② The owner of the store has been teaching how to make delicious bagels to the local people since he opened the store.
　③ The owner of the store wants people with the same background to share their love for bagels.
　④ The owner of the store was taught how to make delicious bagels by the local people.

Which opinion do you agree with? // Why? //

Having cats as pets / will cause you less trouble. // You don't have to take your cat / for a walk. // When cats go to the bathroom, / they just take care of themselves / by covering their **poo** up. // Also, / having a cat won't put you / 5 in any trouble / with your neighbors / because cats won't bark at / or jump on other people / as dogs sometimes do. //

First of all, / dogs can be trained / to help human beings / in many ways. // We have **therapy** dogs, / guide dogs, / and even rescue dogs. // Moreover, / walking your dog every day / will surely help you stay healthy. // Above all, / 10 dogs are much more **sociable** / and **affectionate** toward us / than cats. // You know, / dogs have long been called "man's best friend." //

(129 words)

🔊)) **音読しよう** 　　　　　　　　　　　　　　　　　　スピーキング・トレーナー

Practice 1　スラッシュ位置で文を区切って読んでみよう ☐
Practice 2　音声を聞きながら，音声のすぐ後を追って読んでみよう ☐
TRY!　1分10秒以内に本文全体を音読しよう ☐

📖 **Reading**　本文の内容を読んで理解しよう【知識・技能】【思考力・判断力・表現力】　　共通テスト GTEC®

Make the correct choice to complete each sentence or answer each question.　(各5点[(3)は完答])

(1) What does "man" mean in line 11?　☐

　① human　　　　　② husband　　　　　③ male　　　　　④ grown-up

(2) With training, ☐.

　① cats become able to rescue or guide people

　② cats become able to take care of themselves

　③ dogs become able to cover their poo up

　④ dogs become able to rescue or guide people

(3) Which of the following are true? (Choose two options. The order does not matter.)
☐ · ☐

　① Cats are much more sociable and affectionate toward people than dogs.

　② Dogs don't bark at or jump on other people like cats do.

　③ Taking a dog for a walk can help people stay healthy.

　④ There are therapy dogs, guide dogs, and rescue dogs.

　⑤ We call cats "man's best friend."

A Drone Changed My Life

教科書 p. 186　　/ 15

Interviewer: Please tell me / about how you got into flying drones. //

Tomoki: When I was in junior high school, / I saw an exciting video **clip** / made with drones / on the Internet. // After that, / I started learning about drones. // **Eventually**, / I **imported** the **components** / for a drone / myself. //

5　*Interviewer:* Wow. // Why did you fall in love / with drones? //

Tomoki: At school, / I was shy / and had few friends. // Flying drones by myself / was a lot of fun. // I started going out / to fly drones / instead of keeping myself at home. // Drones changed my life! //

Interviewer: Tell me more. //

10　*Tomoki:* I took part in international competitions / and performed well. // That gave me **confidence**. // I started a drone company / with my father / and I stopped staying at home. //

Interviewer: What did you learn / from drones? //

Tomoki: Everybody has a chance / to meet something / that can change their life. //

15　*Interviewer:* Well, / thank you very much. //

(142 words)

◁))　**音読しよう** 📖　　　　　　　　　　　　　　スピーキング・トレーナー

Practice 1　スラッシュ位置で文を区切って読んでみよう ☐
Practice 2　音声を聞きながら，音声のすぐ後を追って読んでみよう ☐
TRY!　1分15秒以内に本文全体を音読しよう ☐

📖 **Reading**　本文の内容を読んで理解しよう【知識・技能】【思考力・判断力・表現力】　　共通テスト GTEC®

Make the correct choice to complete each sentence or answer each question.　（各5点）

(1)　What does "competition" mean in line 10? ☐
　　① combination　　② decision　　③ institution　　④ match

(2)　You have learned that Tomoki ☐.
　　① had a school friend teach him how to fly drones
　　② saw a video clip and became interested in flying drones
　　③ was shy and had no friends
　　④ went shopping for drone parts with his father

(3)　What happened to Tomoki after encountering drones? ☐
　　① He completely lost his confidence in flying drones.
　　② He continued staying indoors just to make drones.
　　③ He founded a drone company all on his own.
　　④ He quit staying at home and went outdoors to fly drones.

Art Doctors

教科書 p. 187

/ 15

Have you ever heard / that there are doctors / in the art world? // Kikuko Iwai, / an art **conservator**, / has restored valuable paintings, / such as Claude Monet's *Water Lilies* / and Vincent van Gogh's *Sunflowers*. // She has also restored some *chigiri-e* paintings. //

5 Iwai says, / "Artworks are alive, / so they are aging / as time passes. // They are extremely **fragile** / and need to be **treated** carefully. // It is essential / to keep their original quality. // I have to choose the best way / to **conserve** the painting / without changing the original message / that the artist wanted to deliver." //

10 Iwai worries / that very few Japanese museums have a special **department** / for art **conservation**. // Kie, / her daughter, / has decided to become an art conservator, / too. // Kie aims to follow her mother's path / as an "art doctor." //

(127 words)

音読しよう　　　　　　　　　　　　　　　　　　　スピーキング・トレーナー

Practice 1　スラッシュ位置で文を区切って読んでみよう ☐
Practice 2　音声を聞きながら，音声のすぐ後を追って読んでみよう ☐
TRY!　1分5秒以内に本文全体を音読しよう ☐

Reading　本文の内容を読んで理解しよう【知識・技能】【思考力・判断力・表現力】　　　共通テスト　GTEC®

Make the correct choice to complete each sentence or answer each question. （各5点）

(1) What does "fragile" mean in line 6? ☐

　① active　　　　　② delicate　　　　　③ simple　　　　　④ solid

(2) An art doctor ☐ .

　① gives medical treatment to staff members working in art museums

　② makes a special department in museums for art conservation

　③ makes replicas of artworks lost in natural or man-made disasters

　④ repairs valuable artworks

(3) Which of the following is **not** true? ☐

　① Iwai believes that artworks are alive, so they are aging as time passes.

　② Iwai tries to choose the best way to conserve the painting without changing the original message.

　③ Iwai worries that no one follows her path as an "art doctor."

　④ Iwai's daughter has decided to become an art doctor.

On the second anniversary / of Pope John Paul II's visit / to Hiroshima / in 1981, / the Monument for Peace was **unveiled**. // The monument is **located** / in the **lobby** / of the Hiroshima Peace Memorial Museum. // The **sculpture** was made / by an Italy-based artist / born in Hiroshima. // It is 3 meters high, / 1.8

5 meters wide, / and 0.9 meters long. // And / it **weighs** 6 tons. // It **symbolizes** the world's **stability**, / harmony / and **coexistence**. //

John Paul II left a powerful **impression** / on Japanese citizens / during his visit. // The Pope made a speech / in front of the Cenotaph for the A-bomb Victims / on February 25, 1981. // He read his appeal **aloud** / in nine languages, /

10 including Japanese. // His words called on the world / to abolish nuclear weapons. // A passage / from his appeal / is **inscribed** / on the monument, / both in Japanese and in English. //

(136 words)

🔊 **音読しよう** 📖 ～～～～～～～～～～～～～～ **スピーキング・トレーナー**

Practice 1 スラッシュ位置で文を区切って読んでみよう ☐
Practice 2 音声を聞きながら，音声のすぐ後を追って読んでみよう ☐
TRY! 1分10秒以内に本文全体を音読しよう ☐

📖 **Reading** 本文の内容を読んで理解しよう【知識・技能】【思考力・判断力・表現力】 〔共通テスト〕

Make the correct choice to complete each sentence or answer each question. ((1)は7点, (2)は完答8点)

(1) The Monument for Peace ☐.
　① is in front of the Cenotaph for the A-bomb Victims
　② is located in the lobby of the Hiroshima Peace Memorial Museum
　③ was made by Pope John Paul II
　④ was unveiled in 1981

(2) Which of the following are true? (Choose two options. The order does not matter.)
　☐ · ☐
　① The monument is 1.8 meters high and weighs 0.9 tons.
　② The monument represents the world's harmony and coexistence as well as stability.
　③ The Pope was an Italy-based artist born in Hiroshima.
　④ The Pope made a speech in Hiroshima in 1981.
　⑤ The Pope read his appeal aloud only in Japanese and English.

Additional
Lesson 9

**Your Ideas May Change
Society**

教科書 p. 189

/ 15

High School Student **Regional** Town **Vitalization** Idea Contest //

　Our town has several challenges / at the moment. // For example, / the population here / has continued to decrease, / **partly** because a lot of younger people leave here / for jobs or higher **education** / when they graduate / from school. //
5　Your ideas can change this situation / and help to achieve future development / of our town. //

　Participants will give a presentation / at the town cultural center / on February 15. // Special prizes will be awarded / to the winners! //

　Application method: / Choose one of the issues below / and **propose** your
10　ideas. // Fill out the **required** online form / by January 31. //
　The **current** challenges / of our town: /
　　1. Health and welfare /　　　2. Cultural **promotion** /
　　3. **Childcare** support /　　　4. Education /
　　5. Environmental measures /　　6. Other //

(124 words)

スピーキング・トレーナー

Practice 1 スラッシュ位置で文を区切って読んでみよう ☐
Practice 2 音声を聞きながら，音声のすぐ後を追って読んでみよう ☐
TRY! 1分5秒以内に本文全体を音読しよう ☐

Reading 本文の内容を読んで理解しよう【知識・技能】【思考力・判断力・表現力】　　共通テスト

Make the correct choice to complete each sentence or answer each question. （(1)は7点, (2)は完答8点）

(1) The purpose of this contest is to ☐．
　① award special prizes to the winners
　② call for ideas to vitalize the town
　③ develop the relationship between the elderly and the young in the town
　④ improve presentation skills of high school students

(2) Which of the following are true? (Choose two options. The order does not matter.)
　☐ ・ ☐
　① Participants of the contest have to give a presentation on all six issues.
　② Participants of the contest need to send the application form by post.
　③ Some participants of the contest may give a presentation on education.
　④ The application deadline is the end of January.
　⑤ The contest will be held on January 15.

Maria Island Pledge

教科書 p. 190 　　/ 15

Maria Island / —— That Is Their Home //

Maria Island sits off the East Coast / of Tasmania, / Australia. // It has a rich natural environment. // Visitors enjoy seeing wildlife / in its natural habitat. // It is a special experience / for everyone / who visits. // Recently, / some photos /
5　visitors have posted / on social media / have made the island known / to many other people. // The number of tourists / has increased greatly. //

One of the most popular animals / among the tourists / visiting the island / is the **wombat**, / an **adorable** and friendly animal. // Sadly, / however, / some people don't recognize / that they are visiting the animals' home. // They often
10　get too close / to the wombats. // The human behavior has a bad influence / on the animals' health. //

Nowadays, / visitors to the island / are encouraged / to sign the Maria Island Pledge. // The pledge begins / as follows: / "I take this pledge / to respect and protect / the **furred** and **feathered** residents / of Maria. // I will remember / you
15　are wild / and pledge / to keep you this way." //

(156 words)

音読しよう　　　　　　　　　　　　　　スピーキング・トレーナー

Practice 1 スラッシュ位置で文を区切って読んでみよう ☐
Practice 2 音声を聞きながら，音声のすぐ後を追って読んでみよう ☐
TRY! 1分25秒以内に本文全体を音読しよう ☐

Reading 本文の内容を読んで理解しよう【知識・技能】【思考力・判断力・表現力】　(共通テスト)

Make the correct choice to complete each sentence or answer each question. ((1)は7点，(2)は完答8点)

(1) The Maria Island Pledge helps visitors to Maria Island ☐.

① realize that their behavior has no influence on the wild animals

② respect and protect the wild animals

③ take pictures of the wild animals with them

④ visit the wild animals' habitat and touch them

(2) Which of the following are true? (Choose two options. The order does not matter.)
☐ ・ ☐

① Maria Island has such a rich natural environment that tourists can enjoy beautiful scenery.

② Maria Island is located on the East Coast of Tasmania, Australia.

③ One of the most popular animals among the tourists visiting Maria Island is koalas.

④ Owing to some photos posted on social media, the number of tourists has increased greatly.

⑤ Visitors to Maria Island are prohibited from entering wombats' habitats.

WPM・得点一覧表

●スピーキング・トレーナーを使って，各レッスンの本文を流暢に音読できるようにしましょう。
下の計算式を使って，1分あたりに音読できた語数 (words per minute) を算出してみましょう。

【本文語数】÷【音読にかかった時間(秒)】×60＝▢wpm

Lesson		WPM	得点
1	Part 1	/ wpm	/ 50
	Part 2	/ wpm	/ 50
	Part 3	/ wpm	/ 50
	流暢さの目安	70wpm	/ 150

Lesson		WPM	得点
2	Part 1	/ wpm	/ 50
	Part 2	/ wpm	/ 50
	Part 3	/ wpm	/ 50
	流暢さの目安	70wpm	/ 150

Lesson		WPM	得点
3	Part 1	/ wpm	/ 50
	Part 2	/ wpm	/ 50
	Part 3	/ wpm	/ 50
	流暢さの目安	80wpm	/ 150

Lesson		WPM	得点
4	Part 1	/ wpm	/ 50
	Part 2	/ wpm	/ 50
	Part 3	/ wpm	/ 50
	流暢さの目安	80wpm	/ 150

Lesson		WPM	得点
5	Part 1	/ wpm	/ 50
	Part 2	/ wpm	/ 50
	Part 3	/ wpm	/ 50
	Part 4	/ wpm	/ 50
	流暢さの目安	80wpm	/ 200

Optional 1		WPM	得点
	Part 1	/ wpm	/ 30
	Part 2	/ wpm	/ 30
	Part 3	/ wpm	/ 30
	Part 4	/ wpm	/ 30
	Part 5	/ wpm	/ 30
	流暢さの目安	90wpm	/ 150

Lesson		WPM	得点
6	Part 1	/ wpm	/ 50
	Part 2	/ wpm	/ 50
	Part 3	/ wpm	/ 50
	Part 4	/ wpm	/ 50
	流暢さの目安	90wpm	/ 200

Lesson		WPM	得点
7	Part 1	/ wpm	/ 50
	Part 2	/ wpm	/ 50
	Part 3	/ wpm	/ 50
	Part 4	/ wpm	/ 50
	流暢さの目安	90wpm	/ 200

Lesson		WPM	得点
8	Part 1	/ wpm	/ 50
	Part 2	/ wpm	/ 50
	Part 3	/ wpm	/ 50
	Part 4	/ wpm	/ 50
	流暢さの目安	100wpm	/ 200

Lesson		WPM	得点
9	Part 1	/ wpm	/ 50
	Part 2	/ wpm	/ 50
	Part 3	/ wpm	/ 50
	Part 4	/ wpm	/ 50
	流暢さの目安	100wpm	/ 200

Lesson		WPM	得点
10	Part 1	/ wpm	/ 50
	Part 2	/ wpm	/ 50
	Part 3	/ wpm	/ 50
	Part 4	/ wpm	/ 50
	流暢さの目安	100wpm	/ 200

Optional 2	WPM	得点
Part 1	/ wpm	/ 30
Part 2	/ wpm	/ 30
Part 3	/ wpm	/ 30
Part 4	/ wpm	/ 30
Part 5	/ wpm	/ 30
Part 6	/ wpm	/ 30
Part 7	/ wpm	/ 30
流暢さの目安	110wpm	/ 210

Additional	WPM	得点
Lesson 1	/ wpm	/ 15
Lesson 2	/ wpm	/ 15
Lesson 3	/ wpm	/ 15
Lesson 4	/ wpm	/ 15
Lesson 5	/ wpm	/ 15
Lesson 6	/ wpm	/ 15
Lesson 7	/ wpm	/ 15
Lesson 8	/ wpm	/ 15
Lesson 9	/ wpm	/ 15
Lesson 10	/ wpm	/ 15
流暢さの目安	110wpm	